W9-ARW-111

United States Presidents

Calvin Coolidge

Michael Geoffrey Allen

Enslow Publishers, Inc.

40 Industrial Road	PO Box 38
Box 398	Aldershot
Berkeley Heights, NJ 07922	Hants GU12 6BP
USA	UK

http://www.enslow.com

3 1571 00216 5572

Copyright © 2002 by Michael Geoffrey Allen

All rights reserved.

No part of this book may be reproduced by any means without the written permission of the publisher.

Library of Congress Cataloging-in-Publication Data

Allen, Michael Geoffrey.
    Calvin Coolidge / Michael Geoffrey Allen
        p. cm. – (United States presidents)
        Includes bibliographical references and index.
        ISBN 0-7660-1703-6
        1. Coolidge, Calvin, 1872-1933—Juvenile literature. 2. Presidents—United States—Biography—Juvenile literature. [1. Coolidge, Calvin, 1872-1933. 2. Presidents.] I. Title. II. Series.
    E792 .A79   2002
    973.91'5'092—dc21

                                                      2001004206

Printed in the United States of America

10 9 8 7 6 5 4 3 2 1

To Our Readers:
We have done our best to make sure all Internet Addresses in this book were active and appropriate when we went to press. However, the author and the publisher have no control over and assume no liability for the material available on those Internet sites or on other Web sites they may link to. Any comments or suggestions can be sent by e-mail to comments@enslow.com or to the address on the back cover.

Illustration Credits: Calvin Coolidge Memorial Foundation, pp. 12, 59; Farm Service Administration, p. 99; Library of Congress, pp. 47, 49; Reproduced from the *Dictionary of American Portraits*, Published by Dover Publications, Inc., in 1967, pp. 7, 10, 34, 82, 89; Vermont Historical Society, pp. 17, 21, 55, 67, 68, 70, 73, 75, 78, 81, 85.

Cover Illustration: White House Collection, courtesy White House Historical Association.

Contents

1

HOMESTEAD INAUGURAL

Shortly before 11:00 P.M. on August 2, 1923, Mrs. Perkins, the Western Union telegraph agent in the sleepy town of Bridgewater, Vermont, received some startling news: President Warren G. Harding was dead. After getting over the initial shock, she ran to her husband's bedside and woke him from a sound sleep.

Mrs. Perkins instructed her husband to dress quickly and deliver this monumental news to Vice President Calvin Coolidge, who was vacationing in nearby Plymouth Notch. With the telegraph message still in hand, Mr. W. A. Perkins went to find one of the men in Coolidge's official party, some of whom were staying at a nearby boarding-house.

Vice President and Mrs. Coolidge were enjoying a late-summer vacation at the family homestead. They had arrived on July 8, 1923, intending to spend several well-deserved weeks of relaxation in the quiet, rural

5

atmosphere in which Coolidge had been born and raised. After spending the day on the farm, they retired early each evening, usually around 9:00 P.M.

Arriving in the small village, Mr. Perkins parked in front of the Coolidge Homestead, ran up the granite walkway, and banged on the door. In a few minutes, the door was opened by John Coolidge, Calvin's father. In his hand was a kerosene lamp. Mr. Perkins handed him the telegram, and the vice president's father read it carefully. He then called, in a trembling voice, from the bottom of the stairs to an upstairs bedroom where his son and daughter-in-law were fast asleep.

Recollecting the event in later years, Calvin Coolidge said of the moment, "I noticed that my father's voice trembled. As the only times I had observed that before were when death visited our family, I knew that something of the gravest nature had occurred. . . ."[1]

The message was a tragic one. Warren G. Harding, the twenty-ninth president of the United States, had died from a massive thrombosis, or blood clot, while resting in San Francisco, California. He had been feeling poorly throughout the late spring and early summer, and those close to him—family, friends, political associates—felt he needed a long rest. The relaxed tour of several western states had seemed to be just what he needed. The shocking news meant Vice President Calvin Coolidge was now in effect the thirtieth president of the United States.

Recovering from the immediate shock, Coolidge and his wife dressed slowly, knelt down to pray briefly by their bedside, and then descended to the kitchen. John Coolidge handed his son the telegram officially announcing the president's death. With the president dead, the

President Warren G. Harding (above) died suddenly while on a tour of several western states in 1923. Upon the death of President Harding, Calvin Coolidge became president.

principal order of business was to administer the Oath of Office of the President of the United States to the vice president.

By this time, a number of other individuals had arrived at the homestead. These included Vermont Congressman Porter H. Dale, a close personal friend of Coolidge's, and Joe Fountain, the editor of the *Springfield Reporter* who also represented the Associated Press. Congressman Dale urged Coolidge to take the Oath of Office immediately in order to assure an orderly transition of authority in the United States government.

Traditionally, the oath is administered by the Chief Justice of the Supreme Court. Since Coolidge was not in Washington, D.C., Congressman Dale reminded the vice president that his father, Colonel John Coolidge, was a notary public. Therefore, as a public official, he could legally administer the oath. After checking the Constitution to confirm the exact wording, Calvin Coolidge asked his father to administer the oath in his capacity as a Vermont state official. This was to be the first and so far the only time a father would administer the Oath of Office of the President of the United States to his son.

In what is now identified as the Oath-of-Office Room in the Coolidge Homestead at Plymouth Notch, Calvin Coolidge became the thirtieth president of the United States. The room had a low ceiling and wallpapered walls, a front door, and a set of bay windows looking out on a small front yard. As the center of life for the Coolidge family, the room had been the silent witness to a number of family events and tragedies.

In the book *Homestead Inaugural*, Joe H. Fountain, the only newspaper person at this historic occasion, described the scene in great detail. In his book, *Calvin Coolidge's Unique Vermont Inauguration*, Vrest Orton clarifies much of the legend surrounding this unique event. He describes "the night-time ceremony in a small village house in the remote hills of Vermont, where, by the light of a kerosene lamp, Calvin Coolidge's father administered to his son the Oath of Office as President of the United States."[2]

Witnesses included Grace Coolidge, newspaperman Joe Fountain, Coolidge's personal secretary Erwin Geisser, chauffeur Joe McInerney, Congressman Dale, and L. L. Lane, president of the New England branch of the Railway Mail Clerk's Union. Outside, on the screened porch, stood Herbert Thompson and Dan Barney. Thompson, commander of Post No. 18 of the American Legion, is believed to have accompanied Congressman Dale and Joe Fountain.

A unique moment in history had arrived. Few Americans were aware of the fact that the nation was without a president. At 2:47 A.M. on August 3, Vice President Calvin Coolidge repeated the oath: "I do solemnly swear that I will faithfully execute the Office of President of the United States and will, to the best of my ability, preserve, protect and defend the Constitution of the United States." Then Coolidge added, "So help me God." He was now the thirtieth president of the United States. Following the ceremony, President Coolidge signed three copies of the oath that had been typed by his secretary, Erwin Geisser.

Around midnight, the telephone company had received confirmation of President Harding's death. Knowing that the new president would need access to communication equipment, District Plant Chief W. T. Durfee and Edmond Blake, a lineman, gathered the necessary equipment and

On August 3, 1923, Calvin Coolidge became the thirtieth president of the United States.

headed for Plymouth Notch, arriving around 3:00 A.M. The first telephone was soon installed in the Coolidge Homestead. Within the day, John Coolidge called the central office of the telephone company and asked that it be removed from the homestead. He did not think it would be necessary once his son returned to Washington, D.C.

At 7:00 A.M. the president and first lady sat down to breakfast prepared by Aurora Pierce, the housekeeper of many years. Having slept through all the early morning commotion, she was unaware that she had prepared and served breakfast to the new president of the United States and his wife, Grace Goodhue Coolidge, the new first lady. The breakfast was typical of those consumed by the Coolidge family over the years and included, "rice, wheat cereal, bacon, fried potatoes, rolls and donuts . . . (and) pickles."[3]

United States Marshal Albert M. Harvey had organized a motorcade to escort the new president and first lady to the train depot in Rutland, Vermont. As the official motorcade started toward Rutland, the president ordered a stop at the Plymouth Notch Cemetery. The president and Mrs. Coolidge walked through the cemetery and stood quietly by Coolidge's mother's grave.

On route to the train depot over the narrow and twisting mountain roads, the president's car struck and killed a hog that had escaped its pen. It belonged to Pat Stewart of Mt. Holly, Vermont, whose irritation was soothed by Judge Ernest E. Moore, a member of the motorcade, when he told Stewart to forget the whole thing because "he was probably the only Democrat in history to have a hog killed by a Republican President."[4]

The president, the first lady, and his entourage entered

The new President and Mrs. Coolidge leave Vermont for Washington, D.C., on August 3, 1923.

the private railroad car, maintained by the Rutland Railroad for special occasions, at 9:25 A.M. In an effort to acknowledge well-wishers, to share his grief with the American people at the loss of President Harding, and to assure them that the government was in good and capable hands, the train stopped at every station and flag stop along the railroad route to Washington, D.C.

A newly inaugurated president was on his way to the White House.

2

THE FORMATIVE YEARS: SCHOOL AND WORK

Calvin Coolidge was born on July 4, 1872, in the mountain village of Plymouth Notch, Vermont. He was originally named John Calvin Coolidge in honor of his father, but since everyone called him Calvin, he officially dropped the name John as he got older. At the time of his birth, Calvin's parents lived in a house attached to the local general store and post office. In the immediate vicinity stood the local church, a schoolhouse, and a blacksmith shop. Across the road stood the house and barns of his mother's family, the Moors.

Calvin was born at a time of far-reaching transition in American life. The United States was still in the midst of Reconstruction following the Civil War. Veterans of the Union Army still figured prominently in Fourth of July celebrations, while life for former slaves in the South was little improved. The cigar-chomping Union General

Ulysses S. Grant was near the end of his scandal-ridden time as the eighteenth president of the United States. Despite a strong move toward urbanization, most Americans lived and worked in small towns and villages.

The final settling of the great American West and virtual destruction of Native American tribes were in full swing. Two issues from the Civil War remained unresolved. The position of African-American former slaves in the larger United States society, and how former Confederate states were to be readmitted into the Union, continued to challenge the nation. The Fourteenth Amendment to the United States Constitution, passed in 1866, was supposed to guarantee equality to every citizen, but left out African Americans and women. The Fifteenth Amendment, passed in February 1870, granted African-American men the right to vote but still failed to include women.

The tiny village of Plymouth Notch lay nestled in a beautiful rural setting in Vermont's Green Mountains. With short, hot summers and long, cold winters, daily life was a struggle. Inhabitants enjoyed little time for frivolity. Work was a constant reminder of the difficulties of rural life in Vermont. It was a life that contrasted sharply with growing urban life throughout America where people worked less on farms and more in factories producing consumer goods such as textiles, shoes, clothing, machinery, oil, iron, and steel.

The Coolidge ancestors first arrived in the region near Plymouth Notch around 1781. Calvin's great-great-grandfather, John Coolidge (1756–1822), had served in the Revolutionary War as a captain of American forces. He slowly built up a small farm along the old military road cut by British General Jeffrey Amherst back in the 1750s to connect various British forts.

When Plymouth Township was officially organized in 1787, John Coolidge was chosen as one of the town's three selectmen. It was the selectmen's job to conduct the legal affairs of the town. Thus began the Coolidge family's long and distinguished involvement in local, state, and national politics. This tradition of service was passed down to each succeeding generation of Coolidge children.

Calvin's grandfather, Calvin Galusha Coolidge (1815–1878), and grandmother, Sarah Alemeda Brewer Coolidge (1823–1906) had two sons. The first, Julius Caesar Coolidge, died at the young age of twenty. The second, John Calvin Coolidge (1845–1926), was to become young Calvin's father.

As he grew to maturity, Calvin's father, John, took on a wide range of responsible positions. John's maturity, wisdom, and honesty became known far and wide just as his father's had before him. His willingness to help others was a reflection of his commitment to serving the local and state community. His example of citizenship and community responsibility would eventually rub off on Calvin.

Calvin marveled at his father's knowledge of the traits necessary for survival in their harsh, unforgiving, physical environment. In addition to his sound business judgment, John was skilled with his hands, being an able carriage maker, carpenter, bricklayer, and stonemason. He was also a storekeeper with an excellent "business head," justice of the peace, and representative to the Vermont legislature. Following school in Plymouth Notch and several terms at Black River Academy in Ludlow, Vermont, John Calvin Coolidge settled down at his father's farm in Plymouth Notch to work the land. On May 6, 1868, he married Victoria Josephine Moor, who would become Calvin's mother.

In later years, when the retired president reflected on his early family life on the farm, he said of his father, "If there was any physical requirement of country life which he could not perform, I do not know what it was. From watching him and assisting him, I gained an intimate knowledge of all this kind of work."[1] Throughout his boyhood, Calvin spent a great deal of time with his father. He learned of his father's honesty, willingness to work hard, and, especially, the high esteem and genuine respect everyone held for John Coolidge.

Calvin's mother was a slight woman, who was frequently ill almost from the beginning of her married life. However, she possessed a gentle and sensitive nature. Calvin was especially fond of her. His clearest recollection of her—beyond physical beauty and sensitivity—was that "a touch of mysticism" surrounded her. His mother's ancestors moved to the Plymouth area in the early 1800s. They were farmers who owned land near the Coolidge farm. She was one of six children and had an excellent education (for the times), having completed elementary school and one year at Black River Academy. John and Victoria married on May 6, 1868.

Calvin attended the local elementary school in Plymouth Notch where he earned the reputation as a studious and quiet boy. He skated and went sledding in the winter, tapped maple trees in the maple grove in the early spring, and enjoyed occasional group games during the summer vacation, which extended from May to September. One of Calvin's favorite recreations was to ride

Calvin Coolidge pictured as a young boy.

his horse alone through the meadows around his father's farm. However, in rural farm communities, hard work was generally the order of the day, especially during the short summer months. These days were filled with farm work from sunup to sundown. Despite the hard work, Calvin enjoyed a childhood filled with all the necessities. In fact, the Coolidge family was comfortably well-off for the times, with their own rather large, well-built homestead and farmland from which they drew many of the necessities of life.

In April 1875, Victoria Coolidge gave birth to a girl, Abigail Gratia Coolidge. Abbie and big brother Calvin were very close and enjoyed each other's company. In 1876, their father purchased the farmhouse across the road—the present Coolidge Homestead site in Plymouth Notch. This home remained the property of the Coolidge family until they donated it to the state of Vermont in 1962.

Calvin was also very close with his grandparents. Near the end of his life, Grandfather Coolidge would have Calvin read to him from the Gospel of John. When taking the Presidential Oath of Office in 1925, Calvin would use the same Holy Bible that was always located on a small table in the front room of the homestead. Sadly, when Calvin was barely six years old, his grandfather passed away. His grandfather was to be the first of three family members Calvin would lose before he was eighteen.

Sad as the loss of his grandfather was, the most traumatic loss of Calvin's early life was that of his mother. Victoria Josephine Moor Coolidge was only thirty-nine years old when she died. She had been severely injured as a result of falling from a moving buggy and had never fully recovered. From that time on, she spent much of her time resting in the front room of the Coolidge Homestead. Never in very good health since her youth, she seems to have suffered from lung problems, possibly tuberculosis, that made her a chronic invalid. She spent much time in bed, becoming weaker and weaker over time.

In his later years, following retirement from national politics, Calvin Coolidge vividly recalled the very moment of her untimely death: "When she knew that her end was near she called us children to her bedside, where we knelt down to receive her final parting blessing."[2] Calvin was only twelve. The "greatest grief" he felt with her passing left an emptiness in him that was never quite filled during the remainder of his life. The loss deeply affected Abbie as well, though she seemed better able to bounce back from the tragic loss.

Calvin's boyhood was also a time of political development, the result of attending numerous town meetings and assisting his father in his capacity as justice of the peace and sheriff or constable of the small town of Plymouth Notch. Calvin would eventually put to good use what he saw and heard in his early life because it provided a good working knowledge of the practical side of government. It also impressed on him the importance of proceeding slowly and in an orderly fashion in all governmental activity.

The next phase of Calvin's life propelled him from his quiet, secluded home into the wider world. Though Black River Academy was a mere twelve miles from Plymouth Notch, it was light-years away from life on the farm. At the age of thirteen, Calvin, or "Cal" as a few friends called him, viewed attending the academy as the first great adventure of his life. For him it represented a complete change from the past, something new, and larger and more alluring than his earlier life on the farm. It was full of possibilities and new experiences, in both scenery and people.

There was a Coolidge family tradition at Black River Academy; his father, mother, and grandfather Coolidge had each attended the school for a few terms. Calvin followed a classical course of study at Black River that included Latin, Greek, history, and mathematics. He also studied algebra and grammar, and it was in his study of civil government that he was first introduced to the Constitution of the United States. Near the end of his nearly four years at the school, Calvin also studied rhetoric, ancient history, American literature, geometry, and French.

Life at the Academy, while full of study and classes, was not free from pranks. Though he did not admit a role in the prank, Calvin may have played a part in coaxing a donkey to the second floor. Here is the story in his own words: "One morning as the janitor was starting the furnace he heard a loud bray from one of the classrooms. His investigation disclosed the presence there of a domestic animal noted for his long ears and discordant voice. In some way during the night he had been stabled on the second floor."[3] All he ever said regarding his possible involvement in the matter was to refer to the fact that he was never convicted of participation in this or any other prank and therefore must be presumed innocent.

In the spring of his senior year, tragedy again visited young Cal's life. Following a week of suffering and pain, his sister, Abbie, died at age fourteen. In 1890, medical doctors knew little about her problem, but years later a doctor told

SOURCE DOCUMENT

Ludlow, Vt. Apr. 19 1890

My dear Father

I sent you a card the 17 but did not hear from you yesterday.

I did not get Grandma's letter until yesterday it was missent to the Union.

I hope you are feeling better than you did when I heard from you last.

How do you get along on the cheese-factory?

My oration is all done and about learned the subject is: "Oratory in History" it is about 10 minutes long.

Mr. Sherman told me it was the best one he had seen but I suppose he was flattering me.

If Chapman is coming down to night tell Jennie to send down my clean clothes. I will send up my dirty ones by him Monday.

Would you be willing that I should get a suit of clothes this spring? I hate that I have I have worn every day for almost two terms and do not look hardly fit to wear for best.

Those I got to graduate in I cannot wear until then. Moore has something that suits me just about 17 dollars.

I know my expenses are very large this spring and will get along without a new suit if you think best. Do just as you prefer. Let me know by Chapman if you get this in time.

I am having a very good time this spring but will be glad when I can go home and be with you. It is lonesome here without Abbie.

Love to All,
Calvin.

Calvin wrote this letter to his father while he was away at Black River Academy. He talked about his studies and how much he missed his sister Abbie.

Calvin that he believed she died from appendicitis. Upon being informed by his father of the seriousness of Abbie's condition, Calvin immediately left the academy for the homestead and remained at Abbie's bedside until she died. For the third time in his young life, he had lost a loved one to early death.

Recovering from the pain of the loss, Calvin, then seventeen, returned to and graduated from Black River Academy. Following a summer of work, he prepared to head off to college. Unfortunately, his first experience with college proved short-lived. He contracted a very heavy cold—perhaps the flu—which hindered his performance on the entrance examinations. As a result, he was forced to return home where he slowly recovered his strength.

The following spring he attended St. Johnsbury Academy in St. Johnsbury, Vermont, for one term to further his preparation for college. A successful term of study earned Coolidge an entrance certificate to the fall 1891 freshman class at Amherst College.

During this final summer at home, Calvin again worked on his father's farm. By this time he had fully recovered from his illness and was once again strong and lean. He accompanied his father to the dedication of the Bennington Battle Monument in Bennington, Vermont, on July 4, 1891. The experience left an indelible mark on the young man because, at the event, Cal heard President Benjamin Harrison give the dedication. This man was the first president he had ever seen or heard make an address. He was deeply moved by the experience and wondered how it must have felt to bear the full burdens of responsibility as president of the United States.

3

SEEKING A COLLEGE EDUCATION

I n 1891, Amherst was a small, friendly, quiet college community. Amherst College had been founded in 1821 and originally provided a religious education for men who wished to enter the Christian ministry. By the time Coolidge entered the freshman class, however, the college no longer emphasized its religious focus but had expanded its direction by offering an education in the various liberal arts.

Students were required to attend a daily prayer session and two Sunday services. The small college was a close-knit intellectual community in which faculty and students all knew each other well. Campus life was enriching, stimulating, and challenging for students who took advantage of the opportunity to listen and learn from the high-quality faculty.

With only two dormitories on campus, many students roomed in private houses throughout the local community. Those who could afford the dues and who were invited to pledge lived in fraternities. These fraternities were an important part of the social life of the college and it was important to a student's social life to gain entry into one of the fraternities.

Though Coolidge desired admission to one of the fraternities, he was not selected during "Pledge Week" of his freshman year. Thus he became an "Ouden" or "Barbarian," the names for any Amherst College student not pledged to a fraternity. This situation left him rather unhappy, and when he went home for Christmas break, he was reluctant to return to college. However, he soon put this social rejection behind and returned for his second semester, applying himself to the task of earning a college education.

Failing to secure membership in one of the fraternities as a freshman, Coolidge set about searching for a place to room and take meals while at college. He selected Mr. Trott's house on South Pleasant Street. The upstairs room rented for $60 per academic year, and Coolidge had to provide his own firewood for the wood stove and oil for the kerosene lantern that provided light in the evening. The only other student residing at Mr. Trott's was another freshman from Rutland, Vermont, named Alfred Turner.

Coolidge took his meals in the large dining room of another boardinghouse around the corner from Mr. Trott's. He shared the dining table with several other students. One of them was Dwight W. Morrow, who would play a significant role in Coolidge's later political life. In fact, a number of fellow Amherst College students would later become actively involved in Coolidge's future political life.

Though he was not very successful socially, he did have a good year academically by earning passing grades in all his subjects. Despite his small circle of friends, he had at least three nicknames: Cooley, Cal, and Red.

At the close of the spring term, Coolidge again returned to the homestead to work for his father during the summer. During the busy summer, he got the opportunity to deliver the Independence Day address at local Fourth of July ceremonies. This was also his eighteenth birthday. The speech on "Freedom" was the first of hundreds he would deliver throughout his lifetime. This modest beginning as a speechmaker was the start of a career as a public orator that spanned several decades.

The transition from the safety of the Coolidge Homestead to Amherst College was made easier for Coolidge by his father's marriage to Carrie A. Brown, a local teacher who had never married before. As a graduate of Kimball Union Academy in Vermont, she loved music and books and soon filled the empty place in Coolidge's life due to the loss of his mother. John Coolidge was forty-seven and Carrie Brown was thirty-four when they married. She was an excellent wife and exceptionally devoted stepmother.

While studying philosophy, Coolidge fell under the spell of an excellent teacher, Professor Charles E. Garman. Garman kept students spellbound because he made his students feel that studying philosophy was the most significant part of their college education. Of him Coolidge would later write, "It always seemed to me that all our other studies were in the nature of a preparation for the course in philosophy. The head of this department was Charles E. Garman, who was one of the most remarkable men with whom I ever came in contact."[1]

Coolidge was impressed with Professor Garman because he was a good teacher, and the philosophy of life he taught fit Coolidge's particular view of the universe. Specifically, it was similar to the Congregational-Christian beliefs Coolidge had been taught from early childhood in the tiny Union Church in Plymouth Notch and by his family.

Garman was a somewhat mysterious figure who published religious pamphlets in his basement that were used by students in his sophomore-level philosophy course. He believed and taught that behind the world and all that was in it ". . . there is mind; a conscious, purposive force which directs all processes of universal life."[2] This belief was in keeping with the way Coolidge had been taught to live his life.

Though he was still rather shy, Coolidge proved to his classmates that he had a sense of humor by delivering a very funny speech to his junior class titled, "Why I Got Stuck." The performance—the culmination of an Amherst College tradition—impressed all present and earned him the reputation as a wit. This acceptance would soon lead to the fulfillment of a goal he held since entering Amherst College as a freshman—he was about to be admitted to a fraternity. In his senior year, Coolidge was elected to Phi Gamma Delta. Membership in this fraternity was the highlight of Coolidge's college career and so important to him personally that he remained loyal to Phi Gamma Delta for the rest of his life.

Coolidge was also elected grove orator that year. This required an address to the seniors at Class Day. Coolidge rose to the challenge by delivering a humorous speech with a straight face and successfully made everyone in the room laugh. Even when he was heckled from the audience and asked to repeat one of his sentences, he did so without missing or misplacing a single word. The beginning of his brief speech gives some indication of Coolidge's linguistic and speech-writing ability:

> The mantle of truth falls upon the Grove Orator on condition he wear it wrong side out. For the Grove Oration is intended to give a glimpse of the only true side of college life on the inside. And how can this be displayed but by turning things wrong side out? That is the grove prerogative. We came out of doors to have plenty of room. Reconstructed Amherst has not yet decreed that "fools may not speak wisely what wise men do foolishly." Yet let no one expect that this is an occasion for feeding the multitude on small fishes. I only bring the impressions that we gather by the way, whether they be pleasant as the breath of society roses from over the meadows of Old Hadley, or disagreeable as the ancient odors that filled Athenae Hall.[3]

For the second time in his college life, Coolidge had taken advantage of the opportunity to use his developing public-speaking skills to great effect. Years later, when reflecting on the experience, he said, "While my effort was not without some success I very soon learned that making fun of people in a public way was not a good method to secure friends, or likely to lead to much advancement, and I have scrupulously avoided it."[4]

On Wednesday June 26, 1895, with his father in the audience, Calvin Coolidge graduated cum laude with the Amherst College Class of 1895. There were seventy-six men in the class. About his college career he said,

> In the development of every boy who is going to amount to anything there comes a time when he emerges from his immature ways and by the greater precision of his thought and action realizes that he has begun to find himself. Such a transition finally came to me. It was not accidental but the result of hard work. If I had permitted my failures, or what seemed to me at the time a lack of success, to discourage me I cannot see any way in which I would ever have made progress.[5]

In later years, several of Coolidge's Amherst classmates described him as ordinary, unostentatious, less a talker than a good listener, a man of character, methodical in all activities, constant in his work, determined, simple, and independent. He decided to pursue a law career and discussed options with his father while at the homestead for the summer. At the time, anyone interested in becoming a lawyer faced two study options. He could attend a school of law or apprentice himself to a law firm. Coolidge chose the second option in order to avoid the expense of additional schooling. The process was a practical and inexpensive apprenticeship at a law firm willing to provide the aspiring lawyer a desk and law books. He began his search for a law firm willing to take him on as an apprentice.

4

A YOUNG LAWYER IN NORTHAMPTON

Not too far from Amherst was the somewhat larger city of Northampton, Massachusetts. Near the end of the nineteenth century, Northampton was a thriving trade and industrial hub serving towns in the surrounding area as a center of economic activity. Since it was a county seat for the region, it also contained a county court. As such, the city was a center of local and regional political and judicial activity. Coolidge was familiar with Northampton because Amherst College students often traveled there for dinner or to otherwise enjoy a slice of city life unavailable in the small college town of Amherst.

At the invitation of an Amherst classmate, Ernest W. Hardy, Coolidge had journeyed to Northampton with the objective of meeting with John C. Hammond and Henry P. Field, both Amherst College graduates. These two men operated a very successful law office in Northampton, and were well respected in the community and throughout the state of Massachusetts. They were also active members of the state Republican party and were probably aware of Coolidge's Republican leanings and background.

Upon his arrival in Northampton, Coolidge met briefly with Henry Field, and they shared a brief conversation about the young man's desire to study law under Hammond and Field's guidance. Henry Field was a man of almost as few words as Coolidge, but they understood each other. Field subsequently offered Coolidge the opportunity to occupy one of the empty desks in the office and to begin his study of the law by using the books in their extensive law library. He invited Coolidge to "read as much as he wished and learn what he could."[1]

While the smallness of Northampton offered security and order for its citizens, it was a typical small-city environment in its love of gossip. As a result, everyone knew everyone else's business. Reared in a tiny rural town, Coolidge understood this aspect of small-town life. He was no stranger to gossip and the damage to personal relationships it could cause. He followed his father's example from the very beginning and acted with discreet reserve. This meant that his conduct of everyday affairs was beyond reproach. While he often was forced by circumstances to listen to such talk, he never spread it to others. In short, he minded his own business and let others do the same. Such an attitude earned him a growing reputation as someone who could be trusted with the most private details of a given situation.

With his usual commitment to work, Coolidge devoted the daytime hours to the careful study of law and to the local politics of Northampton. Working every day in the law offices of Hammond and Field from 8:00 A.M. to 6:00 P.M., Coolidge soon became quite knowledgeable about contracts, torts, types of evidence, and issues about real property. He also became increasingly comfortable with court procedures and just how a lawyer was supposed to behave when presenting or defending a client in court. Coolidge became intimately acquainted with the more "practical side of statute law."[2]

After twenty months of studying law books and observing the goings-on in the law offices, Coolidge felt prepared to face the test required for admission to the practice of law in Massachusetts. In those days, the test was an oral one for individuals who studied the law by apprenticeship. With the able assistance of Henry Field, Coolidge appeared before the county committee on June 29, 1897. This committee consisted of judges who practiced law in and around Northampton. The committee members asked Coolidge several questions on the law. His answers to their questions demonstrated that he had indeed studied long and hard and knew the law well. They were satisfied and immediately admitted Calvin Coolidge to the Massachusetts bar, which entitled him to practice law throughout the state.

Just a few days before his twenty-fifth birthday, Coolidge officially became a lawyer. He worked a few more months at the law office of Hammond and Field. He then went his own way, and on February 1, 1898, he opened his own law office. He rented two rooms on the second floor of the Masonic Building in downtown Northampton. Coolidge developed a reputation for consultations that got right to the heart of the problem and offered a reasonable solution for all concerned, "without the danger of being involved needlessly in long and costly litigation in court."[3]

Throughout his youth, Coolidge had been thoroughly imbued with the Republican party perspective. His father, a committed Republican, saw to it that his son learned all about the Republican approach to government. This perspective included a strong belief in minimal government interference in citizens' lives or in the business activities of the nation. Republicans were committed to high protective tariffs, small government, and business as usual. They also championed the nation's return to the gold standard, a complex issue that they simplified by the promise that Republican rule meant economic prosperity for the nation.

As a young lawyer, Coolidge became involved in local politics by becoming an active member of the local Republican City Committee. His view of his own future apparently did not envision much beyond active involvement in the local politics of Northampton. He saw himself as just another country lawyer who might someday end up on the bench as a judge.

Coolidge's political activity began with Henry Field's winning campaign for mayor of Northampton in 1895. Coolidge had helped by passing out ballots to the voters. In the same election, John Hammond, Field's law partner, was elected district attorney. One year later, Coolidge himself was appointed as an alternate delegate to the state Republican Convention. With the election of William McKinley as president of the United States in 1896, Coolidge became an active and regular member of the Republican party.

Calvin Coolidge established a firm Republican-based

political foundation for himself in Northampton over the next several years. In 1897, he became a member of the Republican City Committee for Ward Two, attended a state Republican convention as an alternate delegate, and later was elected Northampton city councilman from Ward Two.

A year later, in 1900, Coolidge ran for the office of city solicitor for Northampton. The city solicitor was the legal advisor to the city council, whose responsibility was to keep the councilmen informed of the legalities surrounding their work on behalf of the city. He was elected to two consecutive terms as city solicitor, but was defeated in a bid for a third. This was the first of only two political defeats Coolidge faced in a long and otherwise successful public-service career.

According to historians,

> In the second year of the presidency of McKinley, American public affairs took a surprising direction. The United States fought a war with Spain and emerged from it as a world power. Whereas the presidential election of 1896 had hinged on the monetary question, that of 1900 was fought on the issue of imperialism.[4]

The United States had, almost overnight, become an imperial power in the world. On the home front, most supporters of imperialism were Republicans while most opponents were Democrats. The nation flexed its military muscles principally in the Pacific, with the annexation of Hawaii and war with Spain. Spain ceded the Philippines for a $20 million payment from the United States. Spain also ceded Puerto Rico and Guam and gave up title to the island of Cuba in the Caribbean Sea.

Teddy Roosevelt became president in 1901 after the death of William McKinley.

In the national election of 1900, McKinley was elected to a second term as president. This second term would be tragically cut short by an assassin's bullet on September 6, 1901. He died on September 14, and Vice President Teddy Roosevelt became president. Though a staunch Republican who believed in smaller government, President Roosevelt was responsible for enlarging the office of president of the United States. He loved being president, enjoyed the power and public adulation, and was a larger-than-life type of character. His "Big Stick" and "Square Deal" policies were designed to expand the power of national government and its role in the lives of all Americans. This was especially true on the domestic scene in his attempts to reign in the worst excesses of "Big Business" through various government-run regulatory controls on the food and drug industries. On the foreign scene, he was an imperialist who had fought in the Spanish-American War. Throughout this time, Coolidge worked quietly and efficiently at his growing law practice while keeping an eye on the national political scene.

On June 4, 1903, Coolidge was appointed to fill the vacant position of clerk of courts for Northampton after the previous clerk died while in office. At the end of his appointed term, Coolidge decided not to run for election. He had decided instead to return to private law practice and continue his involvement in local Republican politics in Northampton. Though the position of clerk of courts offered a steady income, Coolidge saw no real political future in it for himself. The practice of law offered less money but greater possibilities for service to the community and for forging important political connections.

In 1905, Coolidge worked hard to get a Republican elected as mayor of Northampton and was rather disappointed when his candidate lost. However, he had learned a valuable lesson in the campaign that he never forgot. During the campaign, Coolidge and others campaigning for the Republican candidate spent too much time talking about the problems of their opponent and too little time discussing what their candidate could offer voters. In other words, it was a negative campaign waged against the Democratic candidate much more than it was a positive campaign for the Republican candidate. Voters saw through the negative campaign and voted for the Democratic candidate.

Throughout his childhood and teenage years Calvin apparently never had a girlfriend. He was painfully shy and not very outgoing. Even in college, his various friendships did not include young women. Now thirty-three years old, Calvin Coolidge enjoyed living arrangements similar to those he had experienced in college. In Northampton he roomed in a private house and took most of his meals at Rahar's Inn. As a bachelor he spent his time practicing law and participating in local politics. In his spare time he read and occasionally visited his family in Plymouth Notch. However, this life as a bachelor was about to change.

A local friend, Robert Weir, introduced him to Grace Anna Goodhue from Burlington, Vermont. She had recently graduated from the University of Vermont and decided to attend Clarke School in Northampton so she could learn how to teach deaf children. The two fell in love and got married on October 4, 1905, in Burlington, Vermont. It was the beginning of a long and enduring relationship. They both believed they were made for each other despite their differences—her zest and friendliness offset his shyness. In later years, Coolidge said of their marriage, "For almost a quarter of a century she has borne with my infirmities, and I have rejoiced in her graces."[5]

The Coolidges honeymooned in Montreal but cut their trip short by a week so Coolidge could get back to Northampton to start campaigning for the elected position of school committeeman. At first the couple lived briefly at the Norwood Hotel, then in August 1906 they rented a small duplex house at 21 Massasoit Street, Northampton.

Coolidge lost the election. This was the second election loss Coolidge experienced. It would prove to be the last.

In his first ten years as a lawyer in Northampton, Massachusetts, the young farm boy from Plymouth Notch had built a strong legal reputation and political foundation for himself. He was a successful lawyer, a happily married man, and had won several local elections including city councilman, city solicitor, clerk of courts (by appointment), and chairman of the Republican City Committee. The secret to his political success was in the way he campaigned. Coolidge had formed the habit of personally visiting each constituent and asking for his vote. His request was put in very simple terms. He would simply say, "I want your vote. I need it. I shall appreciate it."[6]

The following month, Coolidge became a family man. John, the first of two sons, was born on September 7,

1906. With the added responsibility of fatherhood and the need to provide for another member of his family, Coolidge continued to work hard at his law practice and to make more and more political contacts through that work. His reputation for quality legal service continued to grow. And his reputation for winning elections as well as unselfish service to the local Republican organization grew as well.

5

UP THE POLITICAL LADDER

For a brief time, Coolidge remained politically inactive but soon decided he would test the political waters again. He decided to run for the elected position of representative in the Massachusetts legislature. Engaging in his usual electioneering style of visiting each voter, Coolidge carried out an intensive door-to-door campaign for votes. Once again his pitch was simple and straightforward. He needed and wanted their vote, so he asked for it. The hard work paid off when he beat his opponent by 264 votes. With the victory, he took the next step up the political ladder. He began to spend his weekdays in Boston, the capital of the state of Massachusetts, and commute home to be with his family on weekends.

Massachusetts had a bicameral, or two-part legislature called the General Court. The lower branch was the house of representatives. The other branch was the state senate. In 1907, the General Court had 240 members, each of whom represented several towns in various regions throughout Massachusetts. Each member of the house of representatives received a yearly salary of $750. The legislative session ran from January through June.

As a new member of the General Court, Coolidge was introduced to the inner circle of the state Republican party. His days were filled with legislative activity and, though an obscure member initially, he soon earned a reputation for trustworthiness and reliability. Throughout the first term he spoke little, listened carefully, and learned much. He narrowly won a second term in the November 1907 elections. During this term in the lower branch of the state legislature, the Coolidge family grew with the addition of a second son. Calvin Coolidge, Junior, was born on April 13, 1908.

At the end of the second legislative session, Coolidge returned home to his family and law practice. But his time away from elective politics would not last very long. By a unanimous vote of the local Republican committee, Coolidge became the Republican candidate for mayor of Northampton. Explaining why he chose to return to local politics after tasting the big times in state politics, Coolidge later said, "I accepted the opportunity, thinking the honor would be one that would please my father, advance me in my profession, and enable me to be of some public service."[1]

In his usual campaign style, he called on numerous voters and sent letters to others. Coolidge said nothing negative about his Democratic opponent Henry E. Bicknell. Rather, he stressed his own prior political experience and record of public service to the city and state. When the election returns were in and all votes counted, Coolidge was elected mayor of Northampton on December 7, 1909, by a majority of 187 votes. Though he did not know it at the time, this election "began a period of continuous office holding which did not terminate until March 4, 1929 at the close of his Presidential term. . . ."[2]

In reporting on his first term as mayor, the local paper listed Coolidge's accomplishments: He had reduced the city debt by $30,000; he had been instrumental in lowering the tax rate from $17 to $16.50 due primarily to his efforts to make city government more efficient and accountable for every dollar spent; teachers' salaries had increased modestly; his administration was credited with faithfully enforcing the local license laws; the efficiency of the fire and police departments had improved; and, finally, a number of important improvements had been made to city streets.

After a second term as mayor, Coolidge decided to once again seek higher political office. He announced his candidacy for the state senate. In a hard-fought campaign, Coolidge was victorious and, once again, was on his way to Boston. Roosevelt was president now, at a time when the Progressive Era, which had its roots in late nineteenth century social, economic, and political reforms, was just beginning to be felt in the United States. "The Progressive Era was a time when Americans sought reforms to curtail poverty, disorder, corruption, and other problems produced by unchecked industrialization, rapid urbanization, and mass immigration."[3]

Roosevelt viewed himself as the president of all the people including laborers and farmers, as well as businessmen. He also made great efforts toward stronger regulatory control of big business. In foreign affairs, President Teddy Roosevelt flexed the nationalistic muscles of the United States by supporting revolution in Panama, which later granted the United States full rights to construct the Panama Canal along a ten-mile-wide strip of land. He was also a strident voice for conservation of natural resources.

Since Roosevelt chose not to run for office in 1909, the Republican party named William Howard Taft as its nominee. Taft won the election against perennial Democratic nominee William Jennings Bryan. Taft would continue some of the progressive efforts of Roosevelt in calling for lower tariffs and antitrust lawsuits against big business. Despite his efforts, he satisfied neither progressive nor conservative Republicans. This continuing split in the Republican party would lead to victory for Democrat Woodrow Wilson in the 1912 and 1916 presidential elections. It would also somewhat affect Coolidge's work in Boston as a state senator.

The highlight of Coolidge's first senate term was the Lawrence Textile Strike. Workers at the twelve textile mills of the American Woolen Company struck over the company's refusal to abide by the new law against hiring workers under the age of eighteen to work more than fifty-four hours per week. The company refused to pay wages for the standard fifty-six-hour workweek to younger workers who could now work no more than fifty-four hours.

The American Woolen Company was one of the largest producers of textiles in the nation. Its factories employed hundreds of workers in working conditions that were dangerous and difficult. Stifling heat in the summer and bone-chilling cold in the winter made such factory work an exceedingly difficult way to earn a living. Between low wages and poor working conditions, the workers finally reached their breaking point. They refused to return to work, and as tensions mounted, the Massachusetts state government felt compelled to step in to avert violence. In an effort to arbitrate the dispute, a committee was formed to work for a settlement agreeable to both employer and employees. As a new state senator, Coolidge's first real test of leadership at the state level came when he was appointed to chair this committee.

As chairman of the arbitration committee, Coolidge's calm manner and unprejudiced position on the issues earned the respect of both factions. By early spring of 1912, the committee had worked out a solution agreeable to both parties. Workers earned a small salary increase and better working conditions and immediately returned to work. The publicity gained by Coolidge in settling the conflict enhanced his reputation for honesty, patience, fairness, and calmness. It may be said that the solutions he supported were at least mildly progressive for the times. Coolidge won a second term as Republican state senator from Northampton.

During his second term, Coolidge chaired the important joint committee on railroads in addition to other duties. This committee was eventually responsible for securing better transportation services and facilities for rural western Massachusetts partly through extending trolley roads to the region. Coolidge was becoming a powerful force in the Massachusetts legislature. Two more terms as state senator followed.

During both terms, he was elected to the post of president of the senate. In his final term, he addressed the senate in a speech entitled, "Have Faith in Massachusetts," which is considered by many to be the best expression of Calvin Coolidge's philosophy of life and politics. In the speech Coolidge stressed the importance of the Commonwealth of Massachusetts when he said,

> This Commonwealth is one. We are all members of one body. The welfare of the weakest and the welfare of the most powerful are inseparably bound together. Industry cannot flourish if labors languish. Transportation cannot prosper if manufactures decline. The general welfare cannot be provided for in any one act, but it is well to remember that the benefit of one is the benefit of all, and the neglect of one is the neglect of all.[4]

Further in the speech, Senator Coolidge reminded those present of the importance of individual responsibility when he said,

> The people cannot look to legislation generally for success. Industry, thrift, character, are not conferred by act or resolve. Government cannot relieve from toil. It can provide no substitute for the rewards of service. It can, of course, care for the defective and recognize distinguished merit. The normal must care for themselves. Self government means self-support.[5]

Finally, near the end of this brief speech, he left listeners with a summary of his vision of life:

> Do the day's work. If it is to protect the rights of the weak, whoever objects, do it. If it be to help a powerful corporation better serve the people, whatever the opposition, do that. Expect to be called a stand-patter, but don't be a stand-patter. Expect to be called a demagogue, but don't be a demagogue. Don't hesitate to be as revolutionary as science. Don't hesitate to be as

reactionary as the multiplication table. Don't expect to build up the weak by pulling down the strong. Don't hurry to legislate. Give administration a chance to catch up with administration.[6]

About the end of his final term in the state senate, Coolidge said, "When I went home at the end of the 1915 session it was with the intention of remaining in private life and giving all my attention to the law."[7] It was not to be. Once again, as before, events interceded to change the course of Calvin Coolidge's life. A gentleman by the name of Frank W. Stearns entered his life, and of all the forces that affected Coolidge's political fortunes, none proved more significant and far-reaching than this man. So far as anyone has been able to determine, Stearns asked nothing in return for the assistance and support he extended to Coolidge throughout the time of their political association.

Born in Boston, Massachusetts, on November 8, 1856, Frank W. Stearns graduated from Amherst College in 1878. He worked in his father's dry goods store. He later became president of the business and amassed a considerable fortune. As a Republican leader in Massachusetts, Stearns was well known among Republican party regulars. His views on Coolidge were also well known. In fact Stearns took considerable ribbing for his strongly held opinion that Coolidge was destined for greatness at some point in his life. While most people who knew him held Coolidge in high personal and political regard, few, if any, believed for one minute that this quiet man from rural Vermont was destined for the greatness Frank Stearns had predicted.

In the belief that Coolidge was destined for greater

things, Frank Stearns devoted himself to promoting the man throughout Massachusetts. It was not long before his efforts began to pay dividends. As the political climate between Republicans and Democrats in Massachusetts and the nation again heated up in 1915, Coolidge announced his interest in the position of lieutenant governor. Meanwhile, Europe had plunged into World War I.

Most Americans were neutral toward the conflict as was President Wilson. Despite this supposed neutrality, American industry benefited from the sale of arms and other war-related material to the British and French. German submarines fired on Allied merchant ships in an effort to halt the flow of war material reaching the Allies in Europe and strained the neutrality of the United States. Among the first Americans to die in World War I were nearly one hundred passengers on the British liner *Lusitania*, which was sunk by German submarines on May 7, 1915. The 1916 presidential election would be directly affected by such events. Most Americans wanted to remain out of direct involvement with the war in Europe, so they were voting in large numbers for politicians who promised continued neutrality.

On the Massachusetts scene, with the help of friends like Frank Stearns, Coolidge's campaign moved into high gear. Throughout the summer primary campaign, Calvin Coolidge delivered speech after speech and, in the end, was nominated as the Republican candidate for lieutenant governor. The Democratic party's promise to keep the nation out of war in Europe was a powerful vote-getter, so the challenge faced by the Republicans in the 1916 election was quite serious. Coolidge's running mate was Samuel W. McCall, the Republican nominee

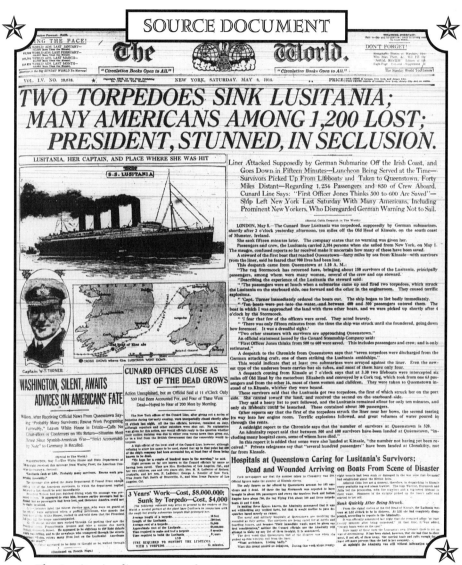

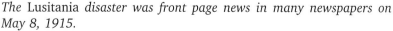

The Lusitania *disaster was front page news in many newspapers on May 8, 1915.*

for governor. On November 2, 1915, the Republican ticket of McCall and Coolidge was elected in spite of major gains by Democrats throughout the nation. For the first time since 1909, Republicans controlled Massachusetts politics. Many felt that newly elected Calvin Coolidge had taken the first steps toward the governor's mansion by winning election as lieutenant governor because this elected position was often a stepping stone to that office. Both men officially took office on Inauguration Day, January 6, 1916.

In his usual manner, Coolidge devoted his time and energy to fulfilling the duties and responsibilities of the high public office. These new duties as second-in-command to the governor forced Coolidge to relinquish much of his law practice in Northampton. Meanwhile, Grace and the two boys, John and Calvin Junior, continued to live in Northampton at 21 Massasoit Street while Coolidge resided at Adams House Hotel when in Boston. He was still able to travel to Northampton most weekends.

During his first term as lieutenant governor, Coolidge spoke frequently throughout the state. As a result of the many speeches, he gained wider recognition, which helped him establish a strong political foundation among supporters and voters around Massachusetts. Coolidge also assisted actively in supporting the war effort on the home front. Though no United States troops fought in Europe in 1916, the nation was actively supplying the Allies with war material at great value to its economy. Coolidge frequently spoke at public rallies urging people to support the war effort in Europe.

As events unfolded in Europe, Germany declared unlimited submarine warfare against all maritime shipping

President Wilson requested a declaration of war on April 2, 1917, and the United States soon entered World War I.

on January 31, 1917. Wilson broke diplomatic relations between the United States and Germany on February 3, 1917. Little more than two months later, on April 6, 1917, Congress adopted the war resolution in response to Wilson's request for a declaration of war on April 2. Wilson believed it was America's duty to preserve civilization and to make the world safe for democracy. The war he had promised to keep the nation out of had claimed another victim. America was again at war.

It was no secret that Coolidge wished to become governor of Massachusetts. His background in local and state politics certainly made him fully qualified. Partway through their third term, Governor McCall informed his lieutenant governor that he had decided not to run for a fourth term as governor. Thus the door was open for Coolidge to campaign.

Coolidge campaigned vigorously for the nomination. After winning the primary, he set his sights on the 1918 general election. With a statewide campaign and continued support of powerful men like state Senator Murray Crane and Frank Stearns, Coolidge won the first of two elections for Governor by a large majority of the Massachusetts voters. The first of Governor Coolidge's two terms was filled with the usual work of the chief executive of a state. Attention to the social, economic, and political needs of the state and its citizens—along with numerous speeches—took up most of his time. His performance in office was a continuation of what citizens had come to expect of Coolidge.

During Coolidge's first term as governor, world events took place that would bear on American life for generations. In October 1917, the Bolshevik Revolution overturned

Czarist Russia and led to a Communist government. Communism would eventually become a major force in international politics. American involvement in World War I cost the lives of many thousands of servicemen. On the domestic scene, Prohibition became the law of the land, and the sale and consumption of alcohol was forbidden. Slightly more than a year later, World War I ended with the signing of the armistice on November 11, 1918.

In 1919, Coolidge was elected to a second term as governor. Once again, he believed he had reached the pinnacle of his political life. The latter portion of his second term, however, proved to be a very different story. America's economy, which had profited mightily from the sale of war material to the Allies, experienced a postwar decline. Returning veterans who had fought bravely in Europe returned home to a stagnant American economy, few jobs, rising prices, and low wages.

Early in January 1919, another textile strike in Lawrence, Massachusetts, came to a head. The American Woolen Company asked Governor Coolidge to send in the state militia to quell the strike. In his usual way, Coolidge sought the widest possible information on the strike situation before making a decision. To secure such information, he personally asked F. F. Fuller on the editorial staff of the *Boston American* to go to Lawrence, at the governor's expense, to assess the real situation. Despite protestations that he favored the strikers, Fuller agreed to make the trip and report back to the governor.

Based on the information supplied by Fuller, Coolidge decided not to send the state militia. What he did do was call the president of the American Woolen Company and urge him to settle the strike. The company took a position of "appeasement" thereby satisfying most of the workers' demands. This event is instructive for understanding that Calvin Coolidge ". . . far from always espousing the cause of the employer, usually preserved a judicial fairness in disputes between capital and labor."[8]

This was not the only strike in the United States during 1919. Labor disputes nationwide numbered around 2,500 with some 4 million workers on strike in some form. The Industrial Workers of the World, the I.W.W., attempted to organize workers into one large union but failed. A major strike of workers in Seattle was suppressed by Mayor Ole Hansen while another, of United States Steel Corporation workers, failed after nearly four months of agitation for better wages and working conditions. In this tense atmosphere, even public employees moved to strike in an effort to secure better wages.

There was quite a bit of pressure throughout the nation to provide jobs for veterans and to raise workers' wages. This pressure was especially strong among public employees such as policemen, firemen, and public transportation workers whose pay had not increased for more than two years. Such economic circumstances soon boiled over into threats and counterthreats between workers and owners and between public employees whose job it was to serve and protect the general public. Workers called for some sort of labor union to protect their interests. Their demands for better pay and working conditions and union representation soon led to riots in Massachusetts and elsewhere. These conflicts would soon have a direct impact on Coolidge's political future in the form of a public employee strike in the city of Boston.

The Boston Police Strike of 1919 proved to be a major

turning point in Coolidge's political career. The publicity surrounding the walkout by Boston police catapulted him into the national limelight. The Boston police were unhappy with their pay, with the meager pay raise offered them by Boston Mayor Andrew J. Peters, and with the general conditions under which they worked. Believing the mayor would refuse what they believed was a fair request for an additional pay raise, the Boston police decided to organize into a union. They saw this move as the only way to secure a more favorable hearing about their grievances. At the time it was against the law for public sector workers to unionize. The police commissioner, Edwin U. Curtis, issued a general order that forbade the police from unionizing. Refusing to adhere to the order, the police applied for a charter from the American Federation of Labor. Hearing this, Curtis issued a counterwarning reminding the policemen that unionization of public employees was illegal. He also reminded them that as public servants they had a duty to the citizens of Boston to remain on the job.

The real trouble began when the American Federation of Labor recognized the Boston police by granting them an official charter. This charter officially recognized the desire of the Boston police to be represented by the labor union. Commissioner Curtis immediately responded by formally charging nineteen senior officers with insubordination.

With tempers on both sides at a fever pitch, any reasonable compromise became increasingly difficult. Initially Coolidge refused to intervene in the dispute, despite numerous requests to do so by various political leaders throughout the state. He felt strongly that the responsibility for dealing with what he judged to be a police matter lay with the commissioner of police.

Finally, with no solution in sight, on September 8, 1919, Commissioner Curtis suspended the nineteen police officers most closely associated with the union drive. By the overwhelming margin of 1,134 to 2, the police department voted to strike the next day. The following day 1,117 policemen followed through on the strike threat and failed to show up at work. With very few policemen still on duty in Boston, chaos and confusion soon reigned. The city was virtually without police protection of any kind. Rioting and looting began to fill the streets of Boston.

Commissioner Curtis initially assured Governor Coolidge that everything was under control. However, the mayor of Boston was not as confident. Fearing further destruction to the city, and in an effort to restore order, Mayor Peters called out the state guardsmen. He also requested additional regiments of guardsmen from the governor. Coolidge agreed and ordered the entire state guard to protect the property and citizens of Boston.

Order was finally restored on September 11. The subsequent firing of all the striking police officers resulted in the president of the American Federation of Labor, Samuel Gompers, sending a telegram to Mayor Peters and Governor Coolidge requesting the reinstatement of the striking policemen. Responding to Gompers, Coolidge said, "There is no right to strike against the public safety by any body, any where, any time."[9] The statement made national headlines. Coolidge's critics attributed his handling of the strike to indecision, while others felt his actions demonstrated a "keen sense of timing." Whatever the truth, Governor Coolidge received "general credit for the restoration of order."[10] The governor fully supported the police commissioner and refused to consider reinstatement of the striking police. They were soon replaced by a whole new force of policemen selected to fill the more than 1,000 positions.

Soon after the Boston Police Strike was settled, Coolidge was elected to a third term of office. Once again his family remained in Northampton so the boys would not have to be uprooted from school. Grace Coolidge spent much more time in Boston with her husband while he was governor than when he was a representative or senator. As the governor's wife, she was expected to attend and host more social functions.

Coolidge, on left in suit, made an inaugural march as governor of Massachusetts.

In 1920, near the end of his third term as governor of Massachusetts, Coolidge received sad news. His stepmother, Carrie Brown Coolidge, had died. She had suffered a long and difficult illness which had begun back in January of the same year. Coolidge had been very close with his stepmother and felt the loss deeply. Following the funeral, Governor Coolidge returned to Boston to finish his final term as governor.

6

MR. VICE PRESIDENT

As presidential nomination time rolled around in the summer of 1920, the name Calvin Coolidge was on the minds of a number of powerful political leaders in the Republican party. After long debates at the Republican National Convention in Chicago, Warren G. Harding was selected as the presidential candidate for the Republican party. The republican leaders then turned toward the job of nominating a vice-presidential candidate. Governor Coolidge's "Have Faith in Massachusetts" speech was circulated among various delegates. Its simple message of hope in the future left a favorable impression on many of them. Also, Coolidge's strong control of the situation during the Boston Police Strike helped his reputation immensely among convention delegates.

With the support of his old friend and colleague Frank

Stearns, Coolidge was officially nominated by Wallace McCamant of the Oregon delegation. Family, friends, former Amherst classmates, and others joined in celebrating Coolidge's good fortune. Though he never actively sought the office, he was prepared to accept the responsibility when the opportunity arose.

Meanwhile, the Democratic party nominated Governor James M. Cox of Ohio as its presidential candidate and Franklin D. Roosevelt as his running mate. The election, in November 1920, ended in a landslide victory for the Republican ticket of Warren G. Harding and Calvin Coolidge. They beat the Democratic ticket of Cox and Roosevelt by some 7 million votes, and with 404 to 127 electoral votes. During his "front porch" campaign, Harding described America's present need as one of healing rather than heroics, normalcy not nostrums, restoration instead of revolution, and serenity in place of surgery. It was just the message people wanted to hear.

On March 4, 1921, Warren G. Harding and Calvin Coolidge took their respective oaths of office as president and vice president of the United States. Calvin Coolidge's wife, Grace, sons, John and Calvin, father, John, and various friends witnessed the event in the United States Senate chamber. The man from the Vermont hills had traveled far from the tiny rural village of Plymouth Notch.

According to the United States Constitution, the vice president's primary responsibility is to preside over the Senate. Beyond this he has few duties. The position paid $12,000 per year and included an automobile and chauffeur. Vice President Coolidge also had his own secretary, page, and clerk and an office in both the Senate Office

Building and the Capitol. Of the first two years in the position, he said, "I was getting acquainted. Aside from speeches, I did little writing, but I read a great deal and listened much. While I little realized it at the time it was for me a period of most important preparation. It enabled me to be ready in August, 1923."[1]

Harding and Coolidge entered office at a major social and economic turning point in the nation's history. By the early 1920s, the United States had become a complex modern society. The economy was booming with automobiles and electrical appliances being produced in record numbers. Watching movies and listening to the radio were

Vice President Coolidge, his two sons, John and Calvin, and his father, John (left to right), at work on the family farm in Plymouth Notch, Vermont.

popular pastimes. Through corporate mergers, a small number of giant companies dominated the industrial base. Labor unions that had managed to gain a foothold during the previous decade declined under strong opposition from employers. The unions had also failed to encourage union membership of African-American industrial workers and the expanding number of women working outside the home. Republicans tried to make business more efficient, responsive to workers and consumers, and profitable through higher protective tariffs, low taxes, and reduced government regulation.

Soon after his inauguration, President Harding called for a series of economic and social changes. With virtually no support from Congress, few of these domestic goals succeeded. During the early 1920s, the United States was readjusting from a war economy to a peacetime one. Unemployment and inflation were high. Thousands of veterans returning from war in Europe faced joblessness or low wages. The situation placed much pressure on local, state, and federal governments to assist people in their efforts to regain the growing prosperity they had come to enjoy before and during the war. Harding's failure to deliver on campaign promises during his first two years in office cost him most of his popularity with voters.

Unknown to both President Harding and Vice President Coolidge, some members of their administration were dishonest. In his post-election haste to reward friends and others who had helped him politically, President Harding made a number of very bad appointments to his cabinet. These men took advantage of their position in the federal government and enriched themselves at the taxpayers' expense. Called his "Poker

Cabinet" because the president and several of these men played poker several times per week, they exhibited a lax and freewheeling attitude toward their responsibilities.

The first scandal to surface was known as "Teapot Dome." Teapot Dome was a region of oil reserves, or domes, near Casper, Wyoming. These oil reserves were supposed to be kept for future use by the United States Navy. While both political parties generally supported the idea of petroleum reserves for defense purposes, there were many private oil interests and politicians who were opposed. They argued that American oil companies could supply the U.S. Navy with all the oil they needed. With the appointment of Senator Albert B. Fall of New Mexico to the position of secretary of the interior under Harding, the Teapot Dome oil reserves were opened to private exploitation through a complex leasing arrangement. Since this action was illegal, it was done secretly by Secretary Fall, who supported private oil interests over the interests of the government.

As part of the arrangement to allow access to the oil, Fall received gifts and "loans" totaling nearly $400,000. Despite attempts to keep this arrangement secret, evidence surfaced by April 1922, which prompted a United States Senate investigation that would last for nearly two years before final resolution. President Harding had stated that the oil leases had been made with his complete and full approval even though he really did not know what was going on within his administration.

Meanwhile, investigation of corruption in the Veterans' Bureau between its head, Charles R. Forbes, and hospital contractors led to Forbes's forced resignation and a subsequent Senate investigation which uncovered fraud, conspiracy, and bribery. Forbes's legal advisor, Charles F. Cramer, committed suicide soon after the investigation of his boss opened.

The knowledge that close friends had betrayed him caused President Harding much grief.

The betrayal by friends and close associates proved too much for him, and his physical health began to decline precipitously. Throughout this difficult period, Coolidge continued to fulfill the duties and responsibilities of vice president. In May, Coolidge took his family to Hot Springs, Virginia for a short vacation, and on July 8, they arrived at the Plymouth Notch homestead to spend a few weeks with Coolidge's father, John.

Meanwhile, Harding had decided to take a trip out west to Alaska and California, so he could get some much needed rest and relaxation. He also felt the need to get out of Washington, D.C., to escape the press and public speculation on his role in the many scandals plaguing his administration. His blood pressure, already dangerously high, went even higher. On the railroad trip across the country, he made dozens of speeches which further eroded his health. Finally, recognizing the seriousness of his condition, the Hardings stopped their tour in San Francisco on July 29, 1923, where the president collapsed in the Palace Hotel.

On the evening of Thursday, August 2, President Harding was in bed recuperating from his collapse. As Mrs. Harding read aloud to him, he suddenly slipped back on his pillow and died almost instantly. He was fifty-eight years old. It was 7:30 P.M. Pacific Time. The Coolidge family was fast asleep in the upstairs bedroom of the Coolidge Homestead, where it was 10:30 at night Eastern Time.

Between 1887 and the evening of August 2, 1923, Calvin Coolidge had earned a high school and college education, prepared for a law career, became active in local politics, established a superb public service record in both local and state government, and, finally, had been elected vice president of the United States. Now Calvin Coolidge's homestead inauguration was about to take place.

In looking back to the events of May 1923, Coolidge described, with a touch of sadness, that final good-bye to the president.

> We left the President and Mrs. Harding in Washington. I do not know what had impaired his health . . . Later it was disclosed that he had discovered that some whom he had trusted had betrayed him and he had been forced to call them to account. . . I never saw him again. In June he started for Alaska and—eternity.[2]

7

THE WHITE HOUSE YEARS

In his autobiography Calvin Coolidge reflected on the challenge of the presidency of the United States when he said,

> It is a very old saying that you never can tell what you can do until you try. The more I see of life the more I am convinced of the wisdom of that observation.
>
> Surprisingly few men are lacking in capacity, but they fail because they are lacking in application. Either they never learn how to work, or, having learned, they are too indolent to apply themselves with the seriousness and the attention that is necessary to solve important problems.[1]

So we see that Calvin Coolidge's work ethic and willingness to do the day's work—coupled with some good fortune along the way—paid off in attaining the highest public office in the land. He not only became president at the death of Warren G. Harding, he earned a four-year term in his own right in the 1924 election.

> To millions of his fellow countrymen who viewed him from afar he seemed the incarnation of common sense and homely wisdom. Most people believed that the country had installed a watchman, who would guard not only against corruption but also against radicalism.[2]

President Coolidge's first order of business was a memorial service and interment for the deceased President Harding. The nation was grief-stricken over the loss of its president despite the scandal that had so deeply tainted the Harding administration. A major reason for these sentimental feelings lay in the belief of the American people that President Harding was not himself a corrupt person. They believed he had been duped by dishonest individuals in both government and private industry. His full role in all these scandals would emerge later and have significant ramifications on the Coolidge White House years.

Little things, that on the surface seemed unimportant, were a part of Calvin Coolidge's first activities as president. He wrote a widely publicized letter to James Lucy, his Northampton shoemaker friend of many years. The letter, though brief, expressed much about the president's sentimental character. In it he expressed his disappointment at not seeing Mr. Lucy recently and the fact that he missed him very much. The president expressed a strong sentimental feeling for the old shoemaker as well as concern for his continued health and prosperity. He also urged the gentleman to take it easy and work less in order to protect his health.

Though not a publicly devout man, Coolidge formalized

his connection with the First Congregational Church in Washington, D.C., when he accepted membership soon after he took office. He realized the importance of membership in a church at this critical time in his life and the life of the nation.

Immediately, citizens began to focus their gaze on the new man in the White House. What was he really like? Would Coolidge be a good president? What was he made of? How did such a man attain the highest office in the land? The answers to these and other questions varied but overall reflected the nation's faith in President Coolidge's ability to lead. It also reflected their recognition of how Calvin Coolidge had conducted himself during other crises. They saw him as solid and reliable and believed he had ". . . enough strength, intelligence, knowledge, and tough-mindedness to run the government."[3]

By 1923 the nation faced a number of domestic and foreign problems and challenges. On the domestic front factory workers faced stagnant wages while wealthier Americans enjoyed good salaries and rising dividends. The mining and textile industries were depressed, while farmers suffered mightily at the hands of new technologies that raised agricultural production but severely depressed farm prices at the same time. Independent farmers were going bankrupt in large numbers. Urbanization continued at a fast pace as people sought better and more secure jobs in the growing industrial centers around the nation.

The foreign challenges included the continuing tensions between America and Japan. War debts payment continued to plague the relationship between America and Europe. The Dawes Plan finally brought a semblance of

Coolidge's wife and two sons, shown here with Coolidge, witnessed the event when he took the oath of office as vice president of the United States.

order to the situation by reducing the bill for German reparations to a more reasonable level than the original figure of $33 billion.

Throughout the autumn, President Coolidge familiarized himself with the daily duties and responsibilities of the Oval Office. For a time, he retained the members of Harding's Cabinet in an effort to maintain continuity in the governing of the nation. Throughout his presidency,

Grace Coolidge added an air of pleasantness to daily events at the White House. Here, she and the president are seen with the White House aides.

Coolidge made "no changes that were avoidable." However, the corrupt people who had flocked to Washington, D.C., during Harding's administration learned quickly that they had no influence over the new president.

With the entrance of the Coolidges, a certain dignity returned to the White House. Speaking of the influence of Grace Coolidge in the early years of their marriage, one author wrote, "Above all, Mrs. Coolidge was amiable. She had the tolerance of an understanding heart. . . ."[4] Gone were the informal ways of President and Mrs. Harding. Grace Coolidge, whom her husband called "Momma," provided an air of dignified pleasantness to the daily events of the White House and was very popular with the people.

Coolidge quickly established a routine from which he seldom deviated during his years as president. Usually out of bed by 6:30 A.M., he took a brief stroll about the White House grounds. He and Grace ate breakfast at 8:00 A.M., after which he proceeded to the office, where correspondence, appointments, and visitors filled the morning. At 1:00 P.M., following a light lunch, Coolidge often napped for one or two hours. It was suggested that this nap proved Calvin Coolidge was a lazy man. Critics overlooked the simple fact that the midday nap was a normal part of farm routine. So it was not unusual for the president to continue the habit. He used good judgment in conserving his energy for important matters and made every effort to see that the work of government was completed in a timely manner.

An interesting aspect of life in the Coolidge White House was their widely known love of domestic pets. They had numerous cats and dogs. The president could sometimes be seen walking around the White House with a big

The president and Mrs. Coolidge had numerous pets. They are seen here with Rob Roy, one of their white collies.

yellow tabby cat draped around his shoulders. However, dogs were the Coolidges' favorite pets. The two most famous were white collies named Rob Roy and Prudence Prim.[5]

The president's first major challenge was a threatened strike by coal miners in the anthracite fields of Pennsylvania. People were concerned with the availability of coal, which at the time was the primary fuel for heating homes. With autumn and winter not far off, Coolidge assured citizens that there would be coal to burn for the winter season. Throughout August 1923, he worked to bring both sides to some sort of agreement by appointing Pennsylvania Governor Gifford Pinchot as special coal-strike mediator. But despite his best efforts to mediate the conflict between miners and owners, the coal miners struck on September 1.

Following continued talks between the two parties, an agreement was reached on September 8 that ended the brief strike. Coolidge's balanced approach to business–labor conflicts once again resulted in workers returning to their jobs. In this case, the miners won their point on wages, which were raised, although working conditions in the coal mines continued to be among the worst in industry.

Soon after the end of the strike, news of the Teapot Dome scandal surfaced in the nation's newspapers. Hearings were held in Washington, D.C., as the full extent of the corruption and graft in the previous administration came to light. Since President Coolidge had no part in the corruption while vice president, he was spared any personal damage, though politically he was forced to demand the resignations of a number of high-ranking individuals in the government and initiate the prosecution of offenders.

Several people were convicted of graft and corruption, and men of prominence in the nation were branded criminals for their illegal behavior. Both civil and criminal suits would last through the rest of the decade. By the time it was all done, the oil reserves were restored to government control, and Secretary Fall would be convicted of bribery, fined $100,000, and sentenced to one year in prison. The manner in which Coolidge handled the crisis restored public confidence in the White House. Given the incorruptibility of the new president, "it is not strange that the grafters and political manipulators who had flocked to

Washington under Harding now saw that their day of glory was over."[6]

For the remainder of the term, President Coolidge presided over the nation in the quiet and efficient manner that was the hallmark of his public service career. In his first message to Congress, and the first to be broadcast over radio, President Coolidge opposed American membership in the League of Nations, although he still favored participation in the World Court of Justice. He believed war debts owed to the United States ought to be paid, though he was willing to adjust the total bill and manner of payment. He was opposed to recognizing the new government of the Soviet Union and supported the strengthening of the army and navy. He closed by reiterating his position on the desirability of tax reduction and opposition to government-based systems of relief or price controls to solve agricultural problems.

During Coolidge's first term as president, tragedy again struck his family. It was to be a tragedy that changed President Coolidge for the rest of his life. In fact, the tragedy would affect him in a way that directly impacted on how he conducted the business of president.

While playing tennis on the White House grounds, Calvin, Jr., had developed a blister on his foot which soon became infected. Blood poisoning resulted and despite heroic efforts by a team of the best surgeons at Walter Reed Hospital in Washington, D.C., Calvin, Jr., succumbed to the poison. On July 7, 1924, after a week of intense suffering, Calvin Coolidge, Jr., died at the age of sixteen. The nation grieved along with the Coolidges. In reading President Coolidge's own words, we get some sense of the enormity of the loss he felt. "In

SOURCE DOCUMENT

THE WHITE HOUSE
WASHINGTON

July 4 1924

My dear Father:—

Calvin is very sick so this is not a happy day for me. He blistered his toe and infection got into his blood. The toe looks all right but the poison spread all over his system. We have five doctors, one from Phila, and 2 nurses. We think his symptoms are a little better now at 1 P M but he had a bad night. Of course he has all that medical science can give but he may have a long sickness with ulcers, then again he may be better in a few days.

We all send our love

Your son

Calvin Coolidge

Coolidge wrote this letter to his father on July 4, 1924, three days before his son died. In it he tells his father that Calvin, Jr., is very ill.

his suffering he was asking me to make him well. I could not. When he went the power and the glory of the Presidency went with him."[7]

According to a recent analysis of the event, the loss of his son was reflected in four areas of the president's life.[8] First, for a few months prior to his son's untimely death, President Coolidge had been especially busy with the duties of his office and with political preparations for the upcoming 1924 election in which he planned to run for the office of president in his own right. Therefore he had very little time to devote to his family, seeing them only infrequently and briefly, usually at the evening meal. This lack of time with both sons came back to haunt the president, as he felt he had neglected his family by giving them too little of his time.

Second, the irony of the power of the presidency was not lost on President Coolidge at the death of his son. While he recognized he was the most powerful person in the nation and probably the world, none of that power could save his son from an early and painful death.

Third, President Coolidge interpreted the death of his son as a sign of punishment for having become president. Apparently, President Coolidge really enjoyed the trappings of the office, such as being the center of attention and the presence of Secret Service men guarding him and his family. He later felt that somehow he was being punished for enjoyment of the high position he had attained.

Finally, the fourth area touched by the loss of Calvin, Jr., lay in his father's loss of interest in the office of president. Though his daily routines remained largely the same, there were subtle changes in his behavior that negatively impacted his daily performance of duties and

Calvin Coolidge, Jr., was laid to rest in the hills of his native Vermont on July 11, 1924.

responsibilities. The president began to let paperwork slide, missed deadlines, and demonstrated less and less interest in the daily job. It was at this time that he began to sleep more, taking longer naps in the afternoon, and retire earlier at the end of the day. For months after the tragedy, Coolidge often would be found sitting in the Oval Office staring out the window toward the tennis court where Calvin, Jr., blistered his foot.

The summer of 1924 witnessed Coolidge's control of the Republican National Convention in Cleveland, Ohio. Still grieving over the loss of his son, President Coolidge did little to secure the Republican National nomination for president. However, due in large part to his popularity, the good economic circumstances of the moment, and his commitment to tax reduction, he easily won the nomination for president in spite of a spirited challenge by the progressivist Robert M. La Follette and Senator Hiram Johnson.

This was a time of Ku Klux Klan resurgence and all the problems brought on by Prohibition. The Democrats, who were deeply divided on these two issues, finally chose John W. Davis as their presidential candidate and Nebraska Governor Charles W. Bryan as his running mate. To further complicate all the political activity, Senator Robert M. La Follette of Wisconsin entered the race as an independent candidate. The disunity of the opposition helped President Coolidge retain the nomination.

After gaining the 1924 Republication nomination for president, the campaign followed. The campaign theme was "Keep Cool With Coolidge." Again the Coolidge candidacy was viewed as preserving the status quo. The campaign motto worked. In this era of prosperity, no one was able to breach the nation's armor of complacency. The

Republican candidates were inaugurated on March 4, 1925. President Coolidge's inaugural speech was the first ever broadcast by radio. Calvin Coolidge had now earned the presidency in his own right.

Coolidge saw the role of government as that of police power, the protection of property and maintenance of public order. A number of observers believed he had very little understanding of the nation's economic system, but his record of cutting taxes and paying down the national debt suggests otherwise. Fortunately, his time while president occurred during high external prosperity. In spite of his hands-off approach to the national economy, President Coolidge received much of the credit for the economic prosperity enjoyed by the nation during most of the 1920s.

Halfway through President Coolidge's term of office, his father, John Calvin Coolidge, died on March 18, 1926. Of his father's passing, President Coolidge said,

> At his advanced age he had overtaxed his strength receiving thousands of visitors who went to my old home in Plymouth . . . I knew for some weeks that he was passing his last days. I sent to bring him to Washington, but he clung to his old home.
>
> It was a sore trial not to be able to be with him, but I had to leave him where he most wished to be. When his doctors advised me that he could survive only a short time I started to visit him, but he sank to rest while I was on my way. For my personal contact with him during his last months I had to resort to the poor substitute of the telephone. When I reached home he was gone. It costs a great deal to be President.[9]

During Coolidge's second term, the economy continued on a boom cycle, unemployment was relatively low, the nation and world were at peace, and the president

Coolidge's father, John, died on March 18, 1926, and was buried in a family plot in Plymouth Notch, Vermont.

continued to argue for lower taxes and less federal control over the daily activities of American citizens. Despite all this prosperity, the inactivity of the Coolidge presidency was not what was needed to stem the rising tide of speculation in the stock market.

The summer of 1927 found the Coolidge family vacationing in the Black Hills of South Dakota, site of the summer White House. It was a time of continued speculation about the upcoming 1928 presidential election and, though President Coolidge was the only logical Republican candidate, he refused to comment on all such speculation. Friends and political allies actively prepared for President Coolidge's expected nomination and campaign. However, it was at this moment that President Coolidge made a dramatic move. The event took place during one of the regularly scheduled press conferences he conducted while at the summer White House.

Twelve words, printed on a piece of paper—"I do not choose to run for President in nineteen twenty-eight" shocked the nation. Only his private secretary, Everett Sanders, knew of the decision before it was announced. Even Mrs. Coolidge knew nothing of the decision until it was announced to the press.

The announcement was made on August 2, 1927, four years to the day that he had become president of the United States in his own right. At the end of his regular 9:00 A.M. news conference, he suggested that news reporters return at noon for another announcement. At the suggestion of Sanders, Coolidge postponed the news of his decision until 3:00 P.M. Eastern Time when the New York stock market closed. Prior to the news conference, Sanders prepared several sheets containing the twelve-word announcement. Coolidge himself passed them out to newsmen in the room. When the door opened, there was a mad scramble to the telegraph lines to file the story.

Coolidge left the press conference with a broad smile on his face. He had caused quite a sensation. Speculation regarding the motives for his decision began immediately. He really believed that almost six years under one man's leadership was enough for the country. He was tired from the burden of the presidency and believed another term would prove difficult for him physically.

Furthermore, he respected the long-running tradition of no third term presidency in the United States. So despite the strong probability of renomination and reelection, Calvin Coolidge closed out his public-service career at the end of his second term as president of the United States.

Soon after this historic announcement, President Coolidge was adopted by the Sioux Indian Nation. He delivered a speech to some ten thousand American Indians and, at their request, donned the native dress given him by the tribe. Frequently criticized for wearing such an outfit in public, the president did so out of respect for the traditions of the Sioux Nation.

During late summer, the Kellogg-Briand Pact was signed on August 27, 1928, in Paris, France, by fifteen nations. Eventually, some sixty-two nations signed the pact that sought to outlaw war as a means of settling international disputes. The treaty was presented to the United States Senate on December 4, 1928, along with a note from President Coolidge requesting that the Senate ratify it before the end of his term in office. The Senate ratified the treaty by a vote of 85 to 1. President Coolidge signed

President Coolidge delivered a speech to the Sioux Indian Nation wearing the native dress given to him by the tribe.

Herbert Hoover defeated Alfred E. Smith in the 1928 election to become the thirty-first president of the United States.

the treaty in a White House ceremony on January 17, 1929. However well-intentioned, the pact did not prevent future wars.

The Republican party met in 1928 to nominate a new candidate for president of the United States. Throughout the convention, many continued to speculate on a possible change of heart by President Coolidge. When they finally realized he really would not accept renomination, Herbert Hoover, who had served as President Coolidge's secretary of commerce, was selected. In the 1928 election, Hoover defeated Alfred E. Smith to become the thirty-first president of the United States.

In his farewell message to Congress on December 4, 1928, President Coolidge warned against extravagance in economics and government. The closing weeks of his administration were uneventful for the Coolidge family as the nation looked forward to the March 4, 1929, inauguration of a new president.

Calvin Coolidge left office as one of the most popular presidents in the history of the nation. On leaving office he said, "We draw our Presidents from the people. It is a wholesome thing for them to return to the people. I came from them. I wish to be one of them again."[10] He looked forward to a quiet retirement back in Northampton, Massachusetts.

8

THE TWILIGHT YEARS

T he Coolidges returned to their old seven-room apartment on 21 Massasoit Street in Northampton on March 5, 1929. They were greeted at the train station by cloudy skies, light rain, and a rather sizable crowd of townspeople and Smith College students. The reception delighted them. After settling into their familiar surroundings, they realized they would have to face a daily and continuous parade of automobiles full of curious sightseers. Even as they rocked quietly on the front porch, people would stop and stare. The quiet retirement they so longed for was not to be.

Within a few months of Coolidge's departure from the highest office in the land, the nation's economy lay in shambles. On "Black Tuesday," October 29, 1929, the Great Depression descended on the nation. The economic situation in the United States saddened Coolidge deeply.

84

Despite this concern, he was no longer in the mainstream of daily public events so was unable to influence the situation in any way.

In the hopes of regaining some privacy, the Coolidges decided to purchase another residence in a quieter neighborhood in Northampton. The house was called The Beeches. It was a twelve-room house on nine acres. The location afforded them a real measure of privacy. Even though it was more difficult for sightseers to bother them in their new surroundings, Coolidge announced in the local newspaper that he did not wish to be disturbed and

The Coolidges moved to The Beeches in order to have more privacy. The house sat on nine acres.

only rarely granted interviews. This notice helped to reduce the number of visitors to their new home.

The peace and quiet the Coolidges had longed for was finally theirs. Prior to his retirement, Calvin Coolidge had completed a draft of his autobiography. It was first published in serial form in *Cosmopolitan* magazine. In book form, it sold well and provided Coolidge with considerable royalties.

Coolidge purchased the Lincoln limousine he used as president and, because he could not drive, employed John Bukosky as chauffeur. Now it was time to find new work. Previous retiring presidents engaged in a variety of business-related activities, often lending their name to various enterprises to make money. In fact, "Coolidge played with the possibility of entering the oil business," but decided against it.[1] To handle a steady flow of mail and correspondence, "The president, as people called him, reestablished himself in his old law office, from which he had never formally departed."[2]

Coolidge arrived at his downtown office in Northampton, Massachusetts, at 9:00 A.M. and worked until noon when he would return to The Beeches for lunch and an afternoon nap. He usually returned to the office in the afternoon and worked until 4:00 P.M. and then took the family dogs for a walk. While at work, he spent his time answering letters and writing a daily newspaper column. The Coolidges traveled occasionally and entertained friends from time to time. It was a slower-paced life that they enjoyed immensely. They spent many hours on the front porch, while their caged canary sang, Coolidge rocked in his favorite chair, and Grace sewed.

In the summers, the Coolidges journeyed to the

Plymouth Notch homestead to escape the Northampton heat. Now accustomed to the conveniences of life, Coolidge had the homestead updated with piped-in water and a modern bathroom. They spent time on the homestead's front porch enjoying the warm sun, clean air, and slow pace of rural village life. Unfortunately, sightseers continued to follow them everywhere and proved bothersome.

On June 30, 1930, Coolidge began writing a series of daily articles that became syndicated throughout the nation. Each article was some two hundred words long and titled, "Calvin Coolidge Says" or "Thinking Things Over with Calvin Coolidge." Topics related to politics, government, and economics. The message was similar to that offered in previous writings and speeches and focused on thrift, hard work, and faith in the future. The column ran for one year from 1930–1931. After a year of enduring the weekly deadline for each column, Coolidge declined the offer to continue the activity.

His work as a director of New York Life Insurance Company proved more satisfying than writing the weekly column. Board meetings were held each month in New York City. During these travels he was constantly hounded by reporters. To their persistent questions he replied, "Nothing whatever to say." Yet they continued to follow him around.

During this same year, Coolidge accepted the presidency of the American Antiquarian Society. He attended every meeting of the society during his three-year term and thoroughly enjoyed the experience. He also became affiliated with the Northampton Literary

Club, which reflected his lifelong interest in reading and good literature.

In June 1931, Coolidge attended the dedication ceremony in Marion, Ohio, for a memorial to the late President Warren G. Harding. He spoke briefly at the ceremony and immediately returned to Northampton. More and more, he found himself quite tired, especially when it came to attending and giving public speeches.

The wear of a busy life began to show on him. Suffering throughout his life from what was called pollen fever, probably a form of asthma, he felt burned out. Despite medical reports to the contrary, he became increasingly concerned with the condition of his heart. It did not help that he had been a cigar smoker throughout his entire adult life.

The June 1932 Republican National Convention in Chicago, Illinois, renominated President Herbert Hoover as the Republican candidate. In an effort to gain support for the nomination, President Hoover asked Coolidge to make a series of speeches on behalf of his candidacy. Despite a growing concern for his health, he accepted the challenge to deliver the series of speeches.

Mr. Coolidge's physical condition continued to deteriorate along with his voice. He managed to deliver one speech in the campaign, at Madison Square Garden in New York City. The speech was broadcast over the radio and was well received. Only with great difficulty was he able to finish the speech. As it turned out, no amount of speech making by the former president would save the Republican party in the 1932 election. The Great Depression had a stranglehold on the nation. Millions of

Franklin D. Roosevelt won the 1932 presidential election.

people were suffering. There were few jobs available and the bread lines were getting longer and longer.

The Republicans lost the election to Democrat Franklin D. Roosevelt, a loss that left Coolidge sad and depressed. He felt out of touch with the times and left out of the business of the nation. He was indeed weary in body, mind, and spirit.

Following the Christmas holiday, Coolidge felt a little better physically. It was important for him to get plenty of rest and not tax his body or mind with politics and speeches. On Thursday, January 5, 1933, the former president experienced another of his periodic attacks of "indigestion" that no one thought much about because they had become frequent. Despite his discomfort that morning, he was back at the office by 8:30 A.M. Around 10:00 A.M., Coolidge told to his secretary that he wished to return home. His indigestion was no better, and suddenly he was again feeling quite ill.

At the entrance gate to The Beeches, Coolidge spoke briefly with Grace who was on her way to town for some shopping. He entered the kitchen, got a glass of water, then descended to the cellar where he checked the coal furnace, and spoke briefly to the gardener. He then went upstairs to his bedroom around noon. In the meantime, Grace had completed her shopping and returned home. A few minutes later, she found her husband dead on the bedroom floor. He had died from a probable heart attack at age sixty.

Memorial services were held in Edwards Congregational Church in Northampton. Approximately thirty-eight thousand people passed the coffin. President Hoover and other high-ranking government members attended the service. Coolidge was buried in the family cemetery in Plymouth Notch, Vermont, beside his father, mother, and second son, Calvin, Jr. Grace would eventually be buried beside her husband.

Coolidge's life was a fruitful one, filled with hard work and years of dedicated public service. In spite of humble beginnings, his confidence and faith, coupled with hard work and a little luck, propelled Calvin Coolidge to the presidency of the United States of America. This accomplishment was indeed a fitting capstone to a life devoted to making other people's lives better.

9
LEGACY

When Coolidge was born, most of the material goods and services often taken for granted today simply did not exist. In 1872, electricity, television, radio, automobiles, instant worldwide communications, grocery stores, department stores, antibiotics, and other wonder drugs were not part of everyday life. Before assessing Calvin Coolidge's legacy, it is important to take a brief look at some of the major changes in American life that transpired between his birth in 1872 and his death in 1933.

In 1872, the nation was still in the midst of Reconstruction from the Civil War. Tremendous growth in industrialization spawned a dramatic increase in urban population as the very nature of work changed. Between 1870 and 1910, for example, more than 20 million immigrants entered the United States. While the immigrants helped meet the insatiable demand for unskilled workers, these same workers began to organize into labor unions to meet the desire of laborers to gain higher wages and better working conditions. By 1900, industrialization and urbanization had effectively transformed American life. While some benefited immensely from this new way of life, many more suffered in poverty. The gap between rich and poor widened substantially in the last quarter of the nineteenth century.

In the area of government, during the years following the Civil War, the presidency was a weak and restricted institution. It has been said that "Presidents of the post-Reconstruction era made little effort to reach out to the public or to exert legislative leadership."[1] Congress was little better. "Its chambers were noisy and chaotic, and members rarely devoted their attention to the business at hand. Instead they played cards, read newspapers, or sent a page to get fruit or tobacco from the vendors who lined the hallways of the capitol."[2] Despite such problems, in the last two decades of the century, Congress had taken the first tentative steps toward federal regulation with the passage of the Interstate Commerce Act in 1887 and the Sherman Antitrust Act in 1890.

Calvin Coolidge was born and reared in a tiny rural, hillside community. This way of life differed dramatically from what was happening in other parts of the nation. The urbanization and industrialization of America had not intruded into Vermont. Life in the state remained pre-industrial, looking more to the past than toward the future.

The Coolidge family was an integral part of that community from the very first Coolidge who settled there back in the eighteenth century. The history of Plymouth Notch and the surrounding area is closely connected to the Coolidge family history even today.

In his youth Calvin earned a classical education, beginning with elementary and secondary school, then college. It was quite unusual for young Americans at the time to graduate from high school and even rarer to go to college and earn a degree. With a clear sense of purpose and a powerful work ethic, Calvin decided not to follow his father into the farming or mercantile business.

The world into which Calvin Coolidge entered as an adult at the turn of the century continued to change at a rapid pace. Republicans were in control of the White House with President McKinley and, later, President Teddy Roosevelt. The pace toward federal regulation quickened under the presidency of progressive-minded Roosevelt in a growing reaction to the laissez-faire economic policies of Republicans, which had prevailed since the late nineteenth century. The first thirty years of the twentieth century proved to be even more tumultuous than the last thirty years of the nineteenth. It was in this environment of social, political, and economic change that Calvin Coolidge lived and served the people who elected him to a series of offices from 1898 through 1928.

As a family, he and Grace passed on to their sons the values they had been taught, including thrift, hard work, responsibility, frugality, and a strong commitment to public service. Before he was thirty years old, Calvin Coolidge had won his first election and, with but two minor exceptions, was to win every office he campaigned for during more than thirty years of public service. The reason for this is simple. He delivered on his campaign promises while conducting the people's business with great care, honesty, integrity, and frugality.

Not once in all of Calvin Coolidge's years in public office was he tainted by scandal or charged with dishonesty of any sort. While any number of people disagreed with various decisions he made, no one ever accused him of taking unfair advantage of his position in public office. He was honest to a fault and the voters knew it. Even as vice president when the Teapot Dome scandal was wreaking havoc on the Harding administration, Coolidge was never accused of collusion in the fraud perpetrated by others in high public office.

There is, however, another side to the story of Calvin Coolidge's presidency. The social and economic problems of the times were such that bold and decisive action on the part of the president and government in general was needed. Given Coolidge's strong belief in limiting government interference in the social and economic life of the nation, such action was not forthcoming. Despite the so-called "Coolidge Boom" during the last eighteen months of his second term, the American economy collapsed soon after he left office. While the economic situation was not his creation, ". . . it arose in an atmosphere of confidence that, under him, the government would impose no obstacles to the expansion of business, the growth of dividends, or stock speculation. He never discouraged speculation, as a man of his prudential nature might have been expected to do, and by certain policies and actions he definitely encouraged it."[3]

Coolidge's record in dealing with racial tensions in the 1920s is one example of his minimalist approach to social problems. Both as vice president and president,

Coolidge urged the creation of various commissions in a genuine effort to improve relations and broaden mutual understanding between the races in the United States. He opposed the "Jim Crow" laws that kept the races segregated, and worked diligently to improve the treatment for African Americans in veterans' hospitals. Coolidge also expressed his disapproval of the Ku Klux Klan in various speeches at Howard University in Washington, D.C.

These actions, however, were simply not enough to reduce long-standing injustices. While by today's standards we may be justified in criticizing President Coolidge for not speaking more forthrightly against the widespread racial prejudices of his day, the quiet way he challenged the racist attitudes of the 1920s placed him somewhat ahead of those times in his attitudes toward race.[4]

In recent years the presidency of Calvin Coolidge and the man himself have been reviewed and reassessed by a number of historians. Coolidge believed strongly in constitutional government. As representative of the people from the local to the national level, he exhibited an unwavering commitment to representative democracy in fulfilling the duties of public office. He was thrifty to a fault, as well as cautious, modest, and rather shy. He was also self-confident, which is an attitude of mind born from his belief in the work he did as a public servant. It has been said that "Coolidge's ordinariness inspired confidence" in the American people.[5]

Probably his greatest accomplishment as President ". . . was his retrieval of public confidence in the office he held."[6] He insisted on ". . . able and economical performance from public servants, by making maximum use of the Bureau of the Budget, and by extending the civil service merit system."[7] While his political relationships with the United States Congress were problematic, he consistently held to fiscal policies that kept down the government budget. Further, he consistently applied any budget surpluses to lowering taxes and reducing the national debt. In both of these efforts, Calvin Coolidge was quite successful. However, given the shaky economic foundation of the nation at the time, with easy credit and rampant speculation in the stock market, the president could have done more to temper such behavior.

Coolidge also worked hard to improve political relations with the Latin American countries. Other accomplishments of his administration included improving relations "with the Philippine Islands, development of waterways [within the continental United States], orderly growth of civil and even military aviation, regulation of radio broadcasting"[8] and other administrative activities that helped to streamline the daily functioning of the federal government.

Many myths closely associated with Calvin Coolidge simply are not true. He has been described so many times as "Silent Cal" that few bother to remember that he delivered literally thousands of speeches during his public service. From his first speech on Independence Day in 1891 to his final speech in support of President Hoover's reelection in 1932, Calvin Coolidge gave more speeches than any of the twenty-nine preceding presidents. He wrote most of those speeches as well. While in the White House he gave monthly radio addresses and averaged nearly eight press conferences per month with newspaper reporters. In fact, it has been suggested that President Coolidge spoke more words to the press than Theodore Roosevelt or Woodrow Wilson. These two presidents were particularly well known for the number of press conferences they held.

As to his supposed lack of humor, it is clear from the record that Calvin Coolidge possessed a dry wit that few really understood or appreciated. From his boyhood pranks on his beloved sister, Abbie, to those times when he would ring the bell calling his staff into his White House office and then hide under the desk just before they entered the room, he enjoyed joking with people. He especially enjoyed exposing the artificial seriousness of very pretentious people, who he believed took themselves much too seriously.

Until the tragic death of son Calvin, Jr., few office holders worked harder or longer than Calvin Coolidge. His reputation for getting the job done was well earned and rightly deserved. However, as described earlier, when young Calvin died, Coolidge seemed to lose all interest in political life. While he neither stopped working nor failed to fulfill the duties and responsibilities of the highest office in the land, his personal energy and political astuteness seemed drained out of him by the loss of his son.

Finally, as to the charge that Calvin Coolidge was responsible for the Great Depression, history clearly shows that in the face of the major concern in the 1920s for making money and promoting continued prosperity, he did what many American people expected—which was to leave well enough alone. However, it must be said that,

> Whether any living statesman could have firmly checked the speculative spirit which engulfed the

Many historians have said that Coolidge contributed to the events of the Great Depression.

American economy at this time is questionable. The fact is, however, that the policies of the administration accentuated the prevailing trend. The President and the Secretary of the Treasury used soothing words when, as we know now, they would have been much wiser to issue warnings.[9]

While it is easy for us to look back on the decade preceding the Great Depression and harshly judge Calvin Coolidge's failure to see the economic disaster ahead, he remained consistent in his commitment to letting people make their own economic decisions. It is by no means a sure thing that anyone could have prevented the Great Depression, even with the high degree of government involvement that exists today. In all probability, more government control of the economy would not have altered the economic consequences of the prosperous 1920s.

Calvin Coolidge was a good son, brother, student, husband, father, and citizen. He was a successful lawyer and public servant because of his consistent commitment to the highest integrity in all his dealings. His is a positive legacy rooted in the values of honesty, hard work, self-discipline, and public service. Today he is considered one of the most popular presidents in United States history and a role model for all those who came after him.

Chronology

1872—July 4: Born in Plymouth Notch, Vermont.

1875—Sister, Abigail, is born in Plymouth Notch.

1877—Begins Village School in Plymouth Notch.

1879—Future wife, Grace Goodhue, born in Burlington, Vermont.

1884—Mother, Victoria Josephine Moor Coolidge, dies in Plymouth Notch.

1890—Sister Abigail dies from appendicitis in Plymouth Notch.

1890—Coolidge graduates from Black River Academy.

1891—Earns a certificate from St. Johnsbury Academy in Vermont for admission to Amherst College; enters the freshman class at Amherst College in Amherst, Massachusetts.

1894—Elected grove orator by Amherst College classmates.

1895—Formally elected to Phi Gamma Delta fraternity at Amherst College; graduates *cum laude* from Amherst College.

1895—Begins the study of law in Northampton, Massachusetts at the law firm of Hammond and Field.

1897—Admitted to the state bar to practice law in the courts of Massachusetts.

1898—Elected to his first public office as member of Northampton City Council from Ward Two.

1900—Elected city solicitor in Northampton.

1901—Reelected city solicitor.

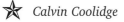

1902—Lost reelection bid for third term as city solicitor.

1903—Appointed as clerk of court for Hampshire County, Massachusetts; meets future wife, Grace Goodhue.

1905—Marries Grace Goodhue at her home on Maple Street, Burlington, Vermont.

1906—The Coolidges move to 21 Massasoit Street, Northampton; elected to Massachusetts House of Representatives; Son, John, is born.

1907—Reelected to Massachusetts House of Representatives.

1908—Son, Calvin Junior, is born.

1909—Elected as mayor of Northampton.

1910—Reelected as mayor of Northampton.

1912—Elected to four consecutive terms in state senate
–1915   and served as president of that body for two terms.

1915—Meets Frank W. Stearns who becomes an important political advisor; elected as lieutenant governor of Massachusetts.

1916—Reelected as lieutenant governor of
–1917   Massachusetts.

1918—Elected governor of Massachusetts.

1919—Gains national prominence by his handling of the Boston Police Strike; reelected as governor of Massachusetts by a record vote.

1920—Receives several votes for the presidential nomination of the Republican party at their national convention; nominated as Republican vice-presidential candidate; elected vice president of the United States by an overwhelming vote.

1921—Named a life trustee of Amherst College.

1923—Sworn in as president by his father at the

Coolidge Homestead upon the death of Warren G. Harding; delivers first annual message to Congress.

1924—Nominated as Republican presidential candidate in his own right; youngest son, Calvin Junior, contracts blood poisoning and dies.

1924—Elected to presidency in his own right.

1925—Chief Justice and former president William Howard Taft administers the presidential oath of office to President Coolidge; new president's inaugural address is first ever to be broadcast over radio to the nation.

1926—Father, John Coolidge, dies in Plymouth Notch.

1927—Delivers the "I do not choose to run for President in nineteen twenty-eight" message to reporters while vacationing in Black Hills, South Dakota.

1928—Delivers short speech from back of train in Bennington, Vermont, extolling the virtues of his home state.

1929—Retires from public office for the last time and returns to Northampton; named a director of New York Life Insurance Company; publishes autobiography; Great Depression begins with stock market crash on Wall Street.

1930—Purchases The Beeches in Northampton to secure more privacy from tourists and onlookers.

1930—Writes newspaper column "Thinking Things Over With Calvin Coolidge."

1933—Dies in upstairs bedroom of a heart attack at age sixty.

Chapter Notes

Chapter 1. Homestead Inaugural

1. Calvin Coolidge, *The Autobiography of Calvin Coolidge* (Rutland, Vt.: Academy Books, Centennial Edition, 1972), pp. 173–174.

2. Vrest Orton, *Calvin Coolidge's Unique Vermont Inauguration* (Plymouth, Vt.: The Calvin Coolidge Memorial Foundation, 1970), p. 7.

3. Ibid., p. 76.

4. Ibid., p. 78.

Chapter 2. The Formative Years: Work and School

1. Calvin Coolidge, *The Autobiography of Calvin Coolidge* (Rutland, Vt.: Academy Books, Centennial Edition, 1972), p. 12.

2. Ibid., p. 13.

3. Ibid., pp. 42–43.

Chapter 3. Seeking a College Education

1. Calvin Coolidge, *The Autobiography of Calvin Coolidge* (Rutland, Vt.: Academy Books, Centennial Edition, 1972), p. 63.

2. William Allen White, *A Puritan in Babylon, The Story of Calvin Coolidge* (New York: Macmillan, 1938. Reprinted by Peter Smith, Gloucester, Massachusetts, 1973), p. 38.

3. *Grove Oration by J. Calvin Coolidge*, The Calvin Coolidge Memorial Foundation, Inc., web site on Early Speeches of Calvin Coolidge.

4. Coolidge, p. 71.

5. Ibid., p. 59.

Chapter 4. A Young Lawyer in Northampton

1. Claude Fuess, *Calvin Coolidge, The Man From Vermont* (Boston: Little, Brown, Reprinted by Greenwood Press Publishers, Westport, Connecticut, 1968), p. 74.

2. Calvin Coolidge, *The Autobiography of Calvin Coolidge* (Rutland, Vt.: Academy Books, Centennial Edition, 1972), pp. 75–76.

3. Ibid., p. 89.

4. Dumas Malone and Basil Rauch, *Empire for Liberty, Volume Two* (New York: Appleton-Century-Crofts, Inc., 1960), p. 195.

5. Coolidge, p. 93.

6. Fuess, p. 93.

Chapter 5. Up the Political Ladder

1. Calvin Coolidge, *The Autobiography of Calvin Coolidge* (Rutland, Vt.: Academy Books, Centennial Edition, 1972), p. 99.

2. Claude Fuess, *Calvin Coolidge, The Man From Vermont* (Boston: Little Brown, Reprinted by Greenwood Press Publishers, Westport, Connecticut, 1968), p. 106.

3. *The American Journey, Interactive Edition*, "Chapter 23: The Progressive Era, 1900-1917" (New York: Prentice-Hall, Inc., 1998), Feature 24, p. 1.

4. Calvin Coolidge, *Have Faith in Massachusetts* (Boston: Houghton Mifflin Co, 1919), pp. 3–4.

5. Ibid., pp. 5–6.

6. Ibid., pp. 7–8.

7. Coolidge, p. 111.

8. Fuess, p. 204.

9. Dumas Malone and Basil Rauch, *Empire for Liberty, Volume Two* (New York: Appleton-Century-Crofts, Inc., 1960), p. 455.

10. Ibid.

Chapter 6. Mr. Vice President

1. Calvin Coolidge, *The Autobiography of Calvin Coolidge* (Rutland, Vt.: Academy Books, Centennial Edition, 1972), p. 165.

2. Ibid., p. 168.

Chapter 7. The White House Years

1. Calvin Coolidge, *The Autobiography of Calvin Coolidge* (Rutland, Vt.: Academy Books, Centennial Edition, 1972), pp. 171–172.

2. Dumas Malone and Basil Rauch, *Empire for Liberty, Volume Two* (New York: Appleton-Century-Crofts, Inc., 1960), p. 452.

3. Donald R. McCoy, *Calvin Coolidge: The Quiet President* (New York: The Macmillan Company, 1967), p. 414.

4. William Allen White, *A Puritan in Babylon, The Story of Calvin Coolidge* (New York: Macmillan, 1938. Reprinted by Peter Smith, Gloucester, Massachusetts, 1973), p. 65.

5. David Pietrusza, *"Wombats and Such" Calvin and Grace Coolidge and Their Pets: The Real Calvin Coolidge* (Plymouth Notch: The Calvin Coolidge Memorial Foundation, Inc., Number 14, 1999), pp. 19–26.

6. Claude Fuess, *Calvin Coolidge, The Man From Vermont* (Boston: Little Brown, Reprinted by Greenwood Press Publishers, Westport, Connecticut, 1968), p. 322

7. Coolidge, p. 190.

8. Robert E. Gilbert, *The Trauma of Death: President Coolidge and the Loss of His Son* (Cambridge, Mass.: John F. Kennedy Library Conference Paper, 1998), p. 6.

9. Coolidge, pp. 191–192.

10. Ibid., p. 242.

Chapter 8. The Twilight Years

1. Robert H. Ferrell, *The Presidency of Calvin Coolidge* (Lawrence: University Press of Kansas, 1998), p. 200.

2. Ibid.

Chapter 9. Legacy

1. David Goldfield, et.al., *The American Journey A History of the United States, Combined Volume* (Saddle River, NJ: Prentice Hall, Inc., 1998), p. 402.

2. Ibid., p. 403.

3. Dumas Malone and Basil Rauch, *Empire for Liberty, Volume Two* (New York: Appleton-Century-Crofts, Inc., 1960), p. 463.

4. Alvin S. Felzenberg, *Calvin Coolidge and Race: His Record in Dealing with the Racial Tensions of the 1920s* (Cambridge, Mass.: John F. Kennedy Library Conference, 1998), pp. 1–11.

5. Donald McCoy, *Calvin Coolidge: The Quiet President* (New York: The Macmillan Company, 1967), p. 413.

6. Ibid., p. 414.

7. Ibid., p. 415.

8. Ibid.

9. Malone and Rauch, p. 461.

Further Reading

Books marked with an asterisk (*) may be purchased from The Calvin Coolidge Memorial Foundation, Inc., Plymouth Notch, Vermont, 05056.

The American Heritage Pictorial History of the Presidents of the United States. New York: American Heritage Publishing Company, Inc., 1968.

Beard, Charles. *The Presidents in American History.* New York: Julian Messner, 1965.

Carmer, Carl. *Pets in the White House.* New York: E. P. Dutton & Company, Inc., 1959.

Coolidge, Calvin. *The Autobiography of Calvin Coolidge.* Rutland, Vt.: Academy Books, 1972, Centennial Edition.*

_____. *The Price of Freedom.* New York: Scribner, 1919.

_____. *Have Faith in Massachusetts.* Boston: Houghton Mifflin, 1919.

_____. *Foundations of the Republic.* New York: Cosmopolitan, 1929.

Fischer, Margaret Jane. *Calvin Coolidge Junior.* Plymouth Notch, Vt.: The Calvin Coolidge Memorial Foundation, Inc., 1981.*

Fountain, Joe. *Homestead Inaugural.* St. Albans, Vt.: The North Country Press, 1950.*

Lathem, Edward Connery, (ed.). *Calvin Coolidge, Cartoons of His Presidential Years.* Plymouth, Vt.: The Calvin Coolidge Memorial Foundation, Inc., 1973.*

_____. *Calvin Coolidge Says.* Plymouth, Vt.: The Calvin Coolidge Memorial Foundation, Inc., 1972*

_____. *Meet Calvin Coolidge, The Man Behind the Myth.* Brattleboro, Vt.: The Stephen Greene Press, 1960.*

McCoy, Donald. *Calvin Coolidge: The Quiet President.* New York: The Macmillan Company, 1967.

Orton, Vrest. *Calvin Coolidge's Unique Vermont Inauguration.* Plymouth, Vt.: The Calvin Coolidge Memorial Foundation, Inc., 1970.*

Ross, Ishbell. *Grace Coolidge and Her Era.* New York: Dodd, Mead, 1962.

Sobel, Robert. *Coolidge: An American Enigma.* Washington, D.C.: Regnery Pub., 1998.

Thompson, Sally. *Growing Up in Plymouth Notch Vermont 1872-1895: The Boyhood of Calvin Coolidge.* Plymouth, Vt.: The Calvin Coolidge Memorial Foundation, Inc., 1972.*

White, William Allen. *A Puritan in Babylon, The Story of Calvin Coolidge.* New York: Macmillan, 1938. Reprinted by Peter Smith, Gloucester, Mass., 1973.*

Places to Visit and Internet Addresses

Calvin Coolidge Homestead Historic Site
Open year-round. P.O. Box 97, Plymouth Notch, Vermont, 05056. (802) 672-3389.

Calvin Coolidge Website and Memorial Foundation
<http://www.calvin-coolidge.org>

The White House–Calvin Coolidge
<http://www.whitehouse.gov/history/presidents/cc30.html>

Vermont Historical Society–Calvin Coolidge
<http://www.state.vt.us/vhs/arccat/findaid/coolidge.htm>
<http://www.state.vt.us/vhs/arccat/findaid/cooladd.htm>

Index

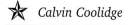